Packin' In On Mules and Horses

SMOKE ELSER   AND BILL BROWN

MOUNTAIN PRESS PUBLISHING CO.
Missoula, Montana
1980

COPYRIGHT 1980
MOUNTAIN PRESS PUBLISHING CO.

Library of Congress Cataloging in Publication Data

Elser, Smoke
    Packin' in on mules and horses.

    1. Packhorse camping.   I. Brown, Bill,
1948-   joint author.   II. Title.
GV199.7.E45   796.54   80-12583
ISBN 0-87842-127-0

MOUNTAIN PRESS PUBLISHING CO.
283 West Front Street • Missoula, MT 59801

Acknowledgements

Pride of authorship can't obscure the fact that many people provided invaluable assistance in the production of this book.

Heading the list of those who merit special thanks are our wives, Thelma Elser and Lynda Brown. Thelma typed the entire manuscript, contributed her years of experience, planning the logistics and food for Smoke's trips, to Appendix I and worked out the details of the diagrams in Appendix II. Lynda read and reread the manuscript and it is better for the many sensible suggestions and her insistance on curbing stylistic excesses. Most of all she was patient and understanding of her husband's frequent absences when the hectic process of finishing kept him out of the house when he should have been home helping her with a new son.

Drs. Jim Brogger and Doug Webber reviewed respectively the material on horse and human first-aid.

Earl Stewart of Stewart's Saddlery and Bob Smith of the Singletree Saddle Shop each contributed invaluable technical information about saddles and equipment.

The photographs simply wouldn't have happened without the advice and assistance of Gordon Lemon and Harley Hettick, though in fairness to these excellent photographers we accept full responsibility for any technical shortcomings in the pictures in this book.

At the eleventh hour, two Missoula businesses, Rosenblum Galleries and The Trailhead, made it possible for us to get essential pictures rapidly.

Others whose contributions transcend any single service are our friends and fellow packers Tom Brown, Deb Chapman, Mike Evans, Robin Pfau and Deloit Wolfe.

Introduction

Packing should be a dying art, but it isn't. There are now more horses in the United States than there have ever been, and many horse owners have begun to realize that old Dobbin is good for something besides a Sunday afternoon pleasure ride or a turn around the show ring. Dobbin can take you places. Packing skills that only a few years ago were preserved by a few old timers and professionals are being mastered each year by growing numbers of enthusiastic, amateur packers.

Unfortunately the ways of packing have been largely an oral tradition, passed on from one practitioner to another. If you live in an urban or suburban area, even in the western mountain states, you may have trouble finding anyone who can teach you the rudiments of packing. We've written this book primarily for people in just that situation, people who own horses and would like to use them for wilderness travel.

Even if you're already a packer, you should find at least some ideas and methods that are new. If you're an elk hunter, a pack horse is the alternative to ferrying quarters on a backpack. We think there's something here too for people who ride into the mountains under the watchful eye of a professional guide or outfitter. If you appreciate the skills and traditions that go into getting you and your gear on a horse or mule and safely down the trail, we think you'll enjoy your experience more than if you are just along for the ride, being deposited at one campsite after another by some reliable old mountain pony. Maybe you're a frustrated cowboy who saddles up a desk chair everyday in New York, Atlanta or Fairbanks. If you've ever longed to get on a horse and ride out of the present for a week, a month or a lifetime, there's fuel here for daydreams.

Enough about you. Who are we? Smoke Elser is a professional outfitter, guide and teacher whose years of experience provide the bulk of the material for this book. I, Bill Brown, am a writer, horseman and mostly amateur packer. I have worked for Smoke as a packer and hunting guide. I asked all the dumb questions that have to be answered in a book for beginners, and I also did most of the writing. This partnership creates stylistic problems whenever we speak of personal experiences. The least cumbersome solution has been for me to refer to myself as I and to Smoke as Smoke. Despite this convention, the book is a joint effort, and whenever possible we speak in unison.

Before we go any further, we want to tell you what this book isn't. It isn't a book on horsemanship. We aren't going to teach you how to ride. If you aren't a rider or are just learning and you're dead set on riding into the hills, go with an outfitter. This isn't a book on camping either. We'll get into some of that, but if you're looking for instruction on how to cook over an open fire, you've come to the wrong place. Finally this book won't equip you to be a professional outfitter. That life holds a romantic appeal for many people, but don't quit your job to take it up just because you've mastered the material in this book. You'll starve.

What we are going to teach you is how to pack with mules and horses, not everything there is to know, but a complete packing system that will get you, your gear and your stock into and out of the backcountry safely and efficiently. Packing is an old business, nearly as old as civilization itself. Over the centuries people have dreamed up hundreds of ways that will work and even more that won't. We're going to show you techniques that will work. We use them. With them you can save yourself and, more importantly, your stock, the agony of trial and error.

The techniques we prefer reflect some regional bias. Because we're from western Montana, we tend to use equipment and methods favored in this country. Don't be too concerned if you're from somewhere else. We try to give an overview, and regional differences aren't that great. You should have little trouble adapting what we teach you to your part of the country.

Eventually you'll settle on packing practices that suit you. Because of this, we've tried to avoid mindless "Do-it-this-way-because-we-say-so" routines. Whenever we tell you that in our experience a particular technique is right or best, we'll try to equip you to form your own opinion.

We'll explain what we're trying to achieve and why we think our way is best. We want you to learn to think about what you're doing and understand it. Packing can't be reduced to formulas. Eventually you've got to be able to solve your own packing problems. Out in the hills you're on your own.

We said that we'd show you how to pack efficiently and since one of the reasons we go to wild country is to escape from the fast pace of our modern world with its mania for efficiency, we'd better say a word in defense of efficient packing. We think efficient packing is a matter of skill and style, not mechanization or shortcuts.

Done well packing can be a source of multiple pleasures. Not only is the partnership between man and pack animal an old one, but images of men with pack animals — the trapper, the prospector, the drifting cowboy — are important parts of our national mythology. There's great satisfaction in mastering a craft that lets you experience, even if only briefly, a bygone way of life.

More tangibly, a pack string can take you into some of the most beautiful wild country left on earth. The pack string has long been a part of the western landscape, and it harmonizes with that landscape. Even the needs of your animals, rather than being a bother or constant preocccupation, can make you more aware of your surroundings: the weather, the quality and abundance of forage, the availability of water and shade.

Once you're in the backcountry a pack string lets you stay there. Aldo Leopold felt that a wilderness experience required an area large enough to "absorb a two weeks' pack trip." That measure is less arbitrary that it might seem, for the experience of wilderness takes time. You need time to change gears, to slow down and forget the office or whether you forgot to turn off the garden hose before you left home. Then you need more time to let the sounds and smells and rhythms of the wilderness take over: changing weather, sun and stars marking off the days, brief glimpses into the lives of wild creatures.

Rewards like these exact a price, and if you pack into the hills, proper care and handling of your stock is part of that price. If every minute of every day is spent loading, unloading, retying shifted loads, replacing shoes, doctoring saddle sores, and then lying awake at night wondering if your string has decided to head back to the truck, you might as well be fighting rush hour traffic. Forget serenity, spiritual refreshment and good fishing. The mountains all around will seem awfully far away.

It doesn't have to be that way. The whole point of going into the wild is to have fun. We want to help you enjoy your ride.

Contents

Figure 1. *A Rocky Mountain canary.*

chapter one
Horses & Canaries

Dawn was breaking over our camp near Hole-in-the-Wall in Montana's Bob Marshall Wilderness. I had heard our friend and neighbor whose pack string we were traveling with, cross the meadow to feed the horses, and I was pulling on my boots to go and help him. My wife Lynda lay beside me in her sleeping bag, just awake enough to be wondering if she would ever walk again. This was her first pack trip, and yesterday we had ridden hard, covering nearly thirty miles and crossing a rugged pass.

A wheezing, warbling resonance wafted through the mist from the direction of our picketed stock.

"What was that?" Lynda mumbled, suddenly more awake.

"A canary," I said, "Go back to sleep."

She did. Everything on this trip was new to Lynda, and she hadn't gotten a straight answer to a question yet. She wasn't about to believe any story about mountain canaries at five in the morning.

Only this wasn't a story. In our pack string we had two, big, mountain canaries, mules named X and Double X. Here in western Montana mules are known as Rocky Mountain canaries because of their irrepressible urge to sing. And a lot of packers in this part of the world think that the best pack horse isn't a horse at all, but one of these big, long-eared birds.

For travel in the mountains, mules probably are the best pack animals. Many people believe that this is because mules can carry more. This is true to a point, but the difference between a horse and a mule of the same size is probably no more than five percent. Shove enough food at him and

a healthy horse or mule can carry a fifth of his own weight 20 to 25 miles a day, day in and day out.

Like many other hybrids, mules exhibit greater vigor than either parent. Mules are tough. They are less prone to disease, and longer-lived than either horses or donkeys. A horse's working life is usually over by age 20, while mules often pack until they are thirty. Horses evolved as animals of the open plains, and the mountains aren't their idea of a good time. Mules travel more easily than horses in the mountains, a difference which shows up clearly when each must pack dead weight. This is largely because horses and mules are put together differently and consequently have different ways of moving. A horse is built along the lines of a frog with long, coiled hind legs for power and shorter front legs for balance and maneuverability. Look at enough horses and you'll see some that seem to slope downhill toward the front. On the level, about sixty per cent of a horse's (or mule's) weight is over his front legs. Downhill the percentage goes up, and to save his knees a horse has to get his hind legs way up under him and take the longest steps he can without interfering with his front feet. The result is a rolling side-to-side gait that a pack picks up and exaggerates. The swaying load makes the horse work harder and makes the saddle and the load harder to keep in the middle of the horse's back.

Even though mules too are built on the frog pattern, they are leveler, with relatively longer front legs. This gives them a smoother way of going, particularly downhill where they take shorter steps and

Figure 2. *Joker, a good type of riding mule.*

Figure 3. *Mules grow attached to the horses they live with.*   Harley Hettick

sway less. Mules also seem to have better balance. Narrower feet and a generally narrower build help them traverse steep terrain where a horse's wider stance and more oval feet are a hindrance. But much of a mule's edge as a mountaineer may be mental. On steep slopes or in heavy deadfall where horses tend to become panicky, a mule merely becomes more intense. Her big ears point forward and she keeps her eyes on what she is doing. Mules can be led safely into country too steep for most horses. This is a real advantage if you plan to pack game on your pack stock.

People who ride mules swear there's nothing better, that changing to a mule is like switching to a Cadillac after years in a Jeep. Unquestionably with their smooth ride and great endurance mules are excellent mounts for many trail riders. Nonetheless we are pushing mules as pack animals not riding stock. Even though many of Smoke's mules can be ridden, we both prefer to ride horses, at least when we have to lead a string. Admittedly this might be mere prejudice or pride — a rider on a mule hardly cuts a dashing figure — but we think we have good reasons.

A mule's placid disposition often masks the fact that she is extremely alert and has a strong urge to look out for herself. Even the most tractable riding mule rarely places the same degree of trust in her rider as a good horse. When things start to go wrong, a mule will often react in unexpected ways and can be slow to respond to her rider. When we've got to move fast to untangle a pack string, catch a loose mule or straighten a pack that has slipped, we prefer a mount that lets us do the thinking. We know lots of wranglers who feel the same.

As pack animals, mules have more going for them than a good suspension system. They have strong straight backs that aren't likely to break down under heavy loads. Handled properly they learn to like people and are easy to catch. That's important in the hills, as is their tendency to quickly become attached to the animals they run with. You can picket your saddle horse, turn your mules loose and get a good night's sleep, knowing that your mules will be there in the morning. Also once a mule has some experience of the world under her girth, she's a pretty calm individual. She isn't likely to shy or bolt when a hat blows off or start bucking when a load slips. Finally because it is a sterile hybrid, a mule won't cause problems in and around mixed strings. A mule's mind is never on the opposite sex, and that's something you can't even say about geldings.

By now you are probably wondering, "If mules are so great, why use anything else?" Mules do have their drawbacks. Not the least of these is that mules are at least potentially more dangerous. Smoke continually reminds his students that all horses and mules will bite, kick and step on you. A horse who kicks usually lashes out blindly. A mule picks her moment, and if she's aiming at your belt buckle, she won't often miss.

Many problems with mules arise because people try to treat them like horses. This mistake is probably responsible for the common conception of mules as ornery, stubborn, and unpredictable. Everyone has seen the old, silent movie where a mule sits down in front of an oncoming freight train and refuses to move. If a mule is stubborn or unpredictable, that usually reflects the way she was trained or handled. The same is true of spoiled horses.

It's important to remember that mules are smart. We don't want to get into an argument about whether horses and mules think, but if they do, mules think more than horses. A mule caught in a barbed wire fence is less likely to tear holes in herself than a horse in the same situation. Once she finds out that struggling hurts, she'll stand and wait for someone to help her. Because she's smart, a mule can't be pushed the way many horses can, though at some point in her education she's likely to test you severely just to see what she can get away with. It's important that you emerge from

this contest of wills as the undisputed boss. Training mules requires both a firmer hand and more patience than training horses, and it takes some experience with mules to hit on the right balance.

Two other idiosyncrasies may make mules undesirable for the casual packer. First, many mules dislike dogs and will attack them. A mule striking with her forefeet can easily kill an unwary dog or a dog cornered along a fence line. Even if you don't own dogs you may want to avoid the consequences of your mule killing or injuring the neighbor's prize Pekingese.

Second, many mules dislike having their feet handled. The mule that will stand quietly to be shod is the exception. Shoeing most mules requires special handling techniques. Many have to be thrown or shod on a table. Before you commit yourself to mules, make sure your farrier is willing and able to work with them.

Mules are expensive, too. In this part of the country a good mule sells for 50 percent to 100 percent more than a comparable pack horse. If you're only going to be a sometime-packer, the difference can be a real savings.

We've made a pitch for mules right here at the start, because of what they can do and because they're often maligned or ignored. But we realize that not everyone has the time or the inclination to learn to work with mules. Occasional packers and family packers with younger children and dogs are well advised to stick with steady, older horses.

We want to keep you thinking about mules though, so we're going to continue talking about them throughout the book. Most of the time, we'll refer to pack stock as mules and riding stock as horses, but often that distinction blurs, so keep in mind that most of what we'll say applies equally to both mules and horses. When it doesn't, we'll say so.

Harley Hettick

chapter two

Pack Stock....From The Inside Out

A pack animal doesn't have to be fast out of the chute, able to do sliding stops, or quick around the barrels. All a pack animal has to do is follow calmly through miles of steep, rugged country, cross down timber, boggy trails, streams and rivers and deliver your gear to camp each night intact. This job requires steadiness and reliability above any other quality, which is why we recommend that you buy pack animals from the inside out.

When you look at a prospective pack horse or mule, the first thing you want to appraise is his disposition and attitude. One of the best ways to do this is to brush him down. This can give you as much insight into his personality as anything else you can do, and while you're at it, you can be looking for signs of injuries and other

defects. By the time you're done, you'll know a lot more about the animal than you would if you stood back and watched while his owner paraded him back and forth. For that matter don't let the seller do anything for you. If you're going to ride the animal, saddle him yourself. Just because his usual handler has no trouble doesn't mean you won't. You want a mule or a horse who trusts people in general and is accustomed to being handled.

You also want him to be easy to catch. This can be hard to appraise in a horse or mule that hasn't been caught or worked recently. Many animals who are hard to catch after a layoff quickly grow accustomed to being caught. They develop a fatalistic attitude toward the person walking up to them with a halter. You can only make your best guess about whether a hard-to-catch animal is going to remain a problem or whether he's only feeling his oats. A horse or mule who merely runs around the corral the first few times you approach, then submits and allows himself to be caught probably won't become a problem. But some animals are genuinely ornery about being caught. If he kicks at you as he goes by or repeatedly turns his tail toward you and lays back his ears when you approach, you'll be smart to write him off immediately. There are enough docile, easy-to-catch animals in this world that there's no need to risk being kicked and injured on a pack trip. And you certainly don't need the aggravation of having each day's departure delayed while you spend an hour trying to catch one animal.

Catching most horses and mules is easier if they don't see you carrying a halter. Like most horsemen, we habitually hold halters behind our backs when approaching an animal. It's doubtful that many are fooled by this, but having the halter behind you may appear less threatening; some animals act as if they fear you'll strike them when the halter is dangling from your side. Hard-to-catch animals who are wise to the halter-behind-the-back trick sometimes can be fooled by buckling the halter around your waist and dropping the lead rope over your shoulder. This lets you approach with your hands empty and in view. Get as close as possible to the horse or mule before reaching out. Then touch him first under the neck or on the chest. Once you've done that you can loop the lead rope around his neck, slide it up to the throat latch and the animal is caught.

The horse or mule should then lead readily and stand quietly while tied. Before you do anything else leave him tied alone for a few minutes and watch to see whether he has any nervous mannerisms: pawing, restless or spasmodic movements, cribbing, or wind sucking. While he's standing look at the place where he eats. If he's tossed his feed around he may be a picky eater. Look also at his pen or stall for signs of cribbing,

Figure 4. A horse or mule isn't caught until you've got the lead rope around his throat latch.

pawing, or kicking. All these things can be signs of a nervous, unpredictable horse. Use good judgement in evaluating what you see. Unused animals when confined often become stir crazy but abandon their nervous tics with work.

After he has stood tied awhile, take a soft brush and begin working on his face. Watch his eyes. Does he look at you calmly or with wide, nervous eyes? Does he act head shy? Many otherwise good mules won't let you touch their ears. Even riding mules sometimes have to be bridled by unbuckling the cheek pieces. You can probably overlook this defect as long as the mule can be haltered easily. You should be less forgiving of a horse with this idiosyncrasy. In the absence of obvious disease, a horse with touchy ears is often spoiled or abused. He's likely to have other undesirable quirks.

While you're at the head, look at the eyes to see if they are clouded. Check for a blink reflex in both eyes. You don't want to buy a blind animal. We know of an old-time horse trader who kept insisting that a horse he was selling "doesn't look right." The buyer, however, was impressed by the horse's excellent conformation and, believing that he was getting the best of the dealer, bought him anyway. Two days later the buyer was back. He had discovered the horse was blind, and he demanded his money back. The dealer refused, saying, "I told you the horse doesn't look right."

Occasionally a mule or horse that's blind in one eye will work out. Like people, they adjust to having only one eye, but, since their eyes are set around to the sides, the problem is more debilitating than for people. You'll have to make a judgment about how well an individual animal compensates. Even in the best of circumstances he'll have to rely on you occasionally to get him through a tough place.

As you work back from his head, keep your free hand against the animal. You'll be able to feel if he is nervous or relaxed. Go over him completely; handle all four feet;

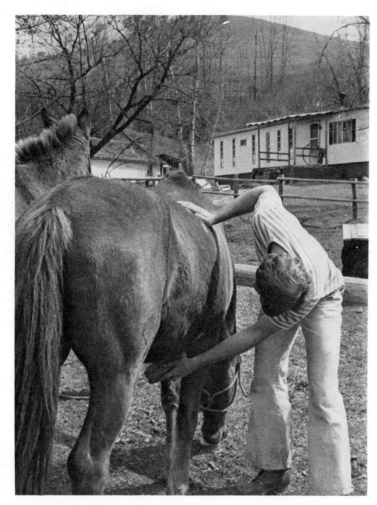

Figure 5. *As you brush, keep your free hand against the animal.*

and keep an eye on his ears and eyes as you work.

Besides brushing the horse or mule, there are some other things you can look at for clues to his personality. A nervous animal often worries too much to get fat. You want your stock to be easy keepers. A little belly isn't a bad thing on a pack animal since rations can be short in the mountains, and the diet can vary a lot from day to day.

Age and the experience that go with it contribute greatly to steadiness. A ten-year-old horse or mule will be calmer and less prone to spook than he was at four. Like people, horses and mules need experience with the world to develop mature good sense. Horses under seven are best regarded as teenagers. Mules seem to mature sooner. Don't pass up an animal that seems perfect for you just because he's smooth mouthed (usually older than eight). Even a 15 year old horse in good condition can give you years of reliable service. Smoke's string contains several veterans who year after year keep their places in the starting lineup even though they are old enough to vote, and I have seen 20-year-old horses perform well in fast, high-goal polo. Except for the race track there's probably no more demanding use that can be made of a horse. Nothing keeps a horse or mule younger than holding down an honest job.

After temperament, the most important part of a pack animal is his running gear, his legs and feet. While you were brushing, you should have been looking these over carefully for splints, puffy knees, swelling, and sidebones. You don't want to find any of these. You do want clean pasterns with no sign of ring bone, and hard, straight tendons with no swelling or fever. If in doubt about your ability to recognize any of these defects, ask your vet to explain them or consult an illustrated veterinary manual.

Generally, a dark colored hoof is tougher than a light one, but look at dark hooves only as a nice plus. Don't reject an animal on the basis of hoof color. It isn't that important. More important is the condition of the hoof. Be wary of extensive cracking and chipping, particularly if the animal is unshod, but consider where he's been pastured in evaluating the seriousness of these conditions. If he's been in a hot, dry pasture, he's likely to have lots of cracks, and if he's been running on rocky ground, his hooves will be chipped no matter how tough they are.

Look too, at how unshod hooves wear naturally. Be wary if a mule or horse is excessively pigeon-toed or duck-footed. A slight amount of either is okay as long as the animal doesn't interfere with himself or seem clumsy. In a young animal such defects can often be remedied over a period of time with corrective shoeing. We don't recommend trying to correct a mature animal unless this is done very gradually and very skillfully. An older animal's muscles, bones and ligaments have matured, and if you suddenly twist the foot around, you're going to hurt him badly and probably permanently. Listen to your farrier's advise on this. Rule out any horse or mule that has foundered or has a constricted frog. The frog of an unshod hoof should contact the ground.

Look at how the horse or mule stands. An animal that has just foundered will not show the characteristic curved and wrinkled hoof for some time, but he'll have very sore front feet, and he'll try to take the weight off them by drawing his hind legs under his belly. A animal thats lame in one front foot will often point with that foot. It's normal for a horse to rest a back leg but not a front leg. Finally, slight lameness which may not show up at a walk can be detected at a trot. A sound horse carries his head on a straight line while trotting. A lame horse bobs. Circle him both ways, and you can tell which side is sore. He'll bob more when circling to the sore side.

A horse's feet should be medium sized in relation to his body. Mules typically have rather small feet. You don't want an animal so heavy in the legs and feet that he's clumsy. Agility is, if anything, more important in your pack stock than in your saddle horse. Led horses come up on obstacles in the trail, like rocks, puddles, or downed trees, quickly and unexpectedly, while a saddle horse sees them well ahead. Even though a pack string is moving slowly, animals on the tail-end experience a crack-the-whip effect on winding trails and switchbacks, and they have to move nimbly to keep up. A pack mule's load is all dead weight, making balance more difficult on steep trails, but the saddle horse can expect help from an alert rider.

If an animal's disposition and running gear check out, it's time to look at his back. In general you want a short, straight back with withers defined enough to hold a saddle easily. Mules have exceptionally straight backs but typically poor withers, so don't set an unreasonable standard. Sway backs or backs that sag in the kidney area are prone to break down. While you were

Figure 6. Rawhide, an excellent type of mule for packing.

9

Figure 7.
Jiggs comes close
to being the ideal
type of pack horse.

brushing, you should have looked for sores or swellings in the saddle and girth area. Patches of white hair on a dark-colored animal indicate underlying scars, and may indicate a tendency to get saddle sores. If you're in doubt, see how the animal's regular tack fits him. A properly fitted saddle may solve all his problems (see the chapter on fitting saddles). If a pack animal is mutton-withered or very round-backed and has signs of girth sores, he's probably very hard to keep a saddle on, and he has sores because he's been cinched too tight. On a high-withered horse look for sores on top. He may be hard to fit with a saddle, though an extra pad often will be all that's needed.

The lower back is common site for injuries. Even sound animals will be more sensitive to pressure here than further forward. Animals loaded with too much weight to the rear develop severe muscle soreness in the kidney area. Over time these same animals often develop spinal arthritis, a chronic condition, as painful and debilitating to a horse or mule as to a

person. This affliction is more common than many people realize since it is often brought about by a combination of poor riding practices and overloaded saddlebags, and it develops slowly. Lower back soreness is not indicative of kidney problems though many horsemen will tell you that it is.

If a horse's or mule's disposition seems to be what you want, and his underpinnings and back are sound and strong, step back and indulge your aesthetic notions of what a good pack horse or mule should look like. Rawhide (Figure 6) is an excellent type of mule. Notice the very straight back. Jiggs, pictured in Figure 7, comes close to being the ideal type of pack horse. For mountain use, powerful, well-muscled hindquarters are highly desirable. So is good wind, and the best indicator of this is a deep — but not necessarily a broad — chest. Lung capacity is a function of the distance from the back to the brisket. Of course a horse or mule with "both front feet coming out of the same hole" may have other problems: he's more likely to interfere with himself, and his balance may not be as good as a slightly more wide-track animal. You don't need a bulldog, though. The neck should be medium length. A pack animal needs enough up there for balance and so he can look around, but not such a long neck that he wants to star gaze and won't watch the ground. An animal with an unusually stubby neck may not keep a saddle in place and may have balance problems. Finally, if you're buying a horse to both ride and pack, short cannon bones often indicate a smoother gait.

We haven't said anything about breeds. This is because we don't believe that any one purebred strain has an advantage over the others for packing, and because grade horses, mongrels, will do a good job for any packer. They're also a lot cheaper. If you already own registered stock, that's fine. We know people who are packing successfully with all of the breeds common in this part of the country. Quarter Horses, Appaloosas, Morgans and even Arabs and Thoroughbreds can make good pack horses, though without good handling and a lot of work, the last two can be a little hot for many people. However, we feel that some Thoroughbred blood in a grade pack horse contributes to size, good withers, finer legs and feet and endurance, and Thoroughbred crosses with any of the breeds listed above generally make excellent mountain horses. We don't recommend the use of American Saddlebreds or Tennessee Walkers. These are specialty horses and not well suited to mountain travel. There's no question that a Walker can cover the miles, but to lead a pack string from one, you're going to need the world's longest lead rope.

You may have noticed that in the last chapter we referred to mules as "she," while in this chapter where we discuss both mules and horses, we've used "he." This is intentional, but not because we are male chauvinists. Most of our favorite mules are females, but we think that you'll have fewer problems with your string if you avoid mares and stick to geldings and mules. A mare in heat is a nuisance in a pack string. It's hard enough to keep several horses' minds on what they're supposed to be doing without having a flirting mare in their midst. At least one of us prefers a mare as a saddle horse, and we realize that you may too. If you already own mares or the best saddle horse you own is a mare, don't go out looking for replacements. But if you're buying new horses for your string, we strongly recommend geldings.

The final thing we want to get you thinking about is size. Bigger is not necessarily better. A thousand pounds to twelve hundred pounds is big enough for most packers. Above twelve hundred pounds you're into the realm of diminishing returns. True, a bigger animal can usually carry more weight, but unless he's well proportioned he may also be more prone to injury. You probably can't use the extra capacity anyway. Remember you have to lift the load. For the average man — say

*Figure 8.
The short packer
on the left
would have
appreciated
a shorter mule.*
USFS

build and temperament. Since they're going to be traveling together, imagine a little POA, a Thoroughbred and a Morgan all in the same string, and you'll see what we mean. One will be too slow, one too fast; another will climb hills better — no one will be happy.

This seems like a good time for a word on mounts for kids. A small horse is better than a pony. Sooner or later you'll want to use him for something else, and a pony won't do. He won't pack much of a load. He probably won't keep up with your big horses, and he certainly won't carry an adult. Rarely are ponies easier for a child to handle; they tend to be willful little blankety-blanks. Even young children can learn to manage an easy-going, smaller horse. In our neighborhood alone there are at least half a dozen kids under twelve who ride full-sized horses with no problems.

A few years ago well-broke, reliable older horses, perfect for packing, were selling for a nickle and a song. Today there is no such thing as a cheap horse. The reason is European and Japanese demand for horse meat. Old Dobbin is going to the canner, not for dog food, but for people food. This has had its greatest impact on the price of the old plug out in the back pasture (registered and performance horses were never cheap), and the stock auctions where most "canners" are sold are no longer particularly good places to pick up pack horses.

160 to 220 pounds and five feet eight to six feet two — a 100 pound load is about as big as he's going to want to lift onto a pack saddle. If you're smaller or a woman, even that's too much. Also, since few of us live right at the edge of the wilderness, we have to ship our horses; a pack horse or mule much bigger than twelve hundred pounds is just taking up extra space in your truck or trailer.

Similar reasoning applies to height. Fourteen hands to fifteen two is a good range for pack stock. Even men over six feet tall are going to find themselves wishing they had a ladder or at least a handy stump to stand on if they start loading animals over 16 hands high. Shorter folks, men or women, will appreciate shorter pack stock.

All of this leads us to perhaps the most important point in selecting pack stock. You should pick your stock to suit yourself, your needs and your string. The needs of the average recreational packer won't be the same as those of a professional outfitter. The professional may be able to use extremely large mules efficiently. The amateur probably won't. Your stock should also be fairly well matched to each other. The interests of harmony are best served if all your animals are about the same size,

You can still get good horses at the sale yards, though, and occasionally a commercial buyer will drop out if they see someone bidding on a sound horse that can be used. At horse auctions, however, you've got to know what you want, and you've got to be willing to take a risk. Auctioned horses come without a warranty, so if you're inexperienced at appraising horses, you may be reluctant to risk several hundred dollars on a horse you know little about. You can minimize the risk by going early and looking over horses that interest you in the stock yards before they go into the ring.

Even if you don't plan to buy, attending a horse sale can be a useful experience. The sale is the best possible place to see a lot of different horses in a short period of time, and because you can run a lot of feet, legs, backs and bellies past your eye, it's a good place to train yourself to look at horses and to refine your tastes. You can also get a feel for what different grades of horses are worth.

Newspaper ads are probably your best source of low to medium priced horses. If you're simply in the market for a pack horse and don't want to spend a small fortune, you can ignore ads that provide a lot of information about the horse. The more in the ad about bloodlines, speed or show results, the more you can expect to pay. Also unless you're a good horseman and have the time to work with an untrained younger horse, you can ignore the ad that reads "green broke, 6-year old gelding" or "spirited mare, well started." These horses are probably a little rank. Instead, look for "family horse" and "horse looking for a good home." It can save you time if height, weight and age are included, though a lot of grade horses never get older than nine.

Probably the only way to get a bargain horse is to find a family that bought a good quiet saddle horse for their daughter Suzy who loved horses when she was 12, but loved boys more when she turned 16. These horses become pets who stand in the

Figure 9. Look for a "family horse," a horse who knows the difference between two kids and three.

Harley Hettick

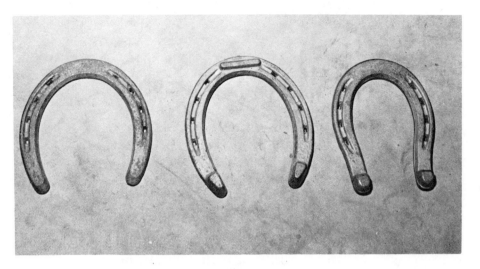

Figure 10.
Types of shoes (l to r):
flat plate;
calked heel and toe;
mule shoe with heel calks.

pasture year after year, eating their way through tons of expensive hay and accomplishing little else. Families are often reluctant to sell their old pets, but they will sometimes sell them cheaply or even give them away if they are sure the horse is getting a good home and if Suzy can retain visiting rights during her vacations from college. You should look such gift horses in the mouth though. If one turns out to be a kicker, a puller, a dog killer, or a gate opener, you've just accepted someone else's headache, and you may not feel that you can turn around and sell the horse that has been so entrusted to your care.

Don't imagine that you can beat the high cost of horses or mules by breeding your own, either. If you want to raise either as a hobby, that's your business, but it's not a cheap way to get into packing. The time between breeding a mare and having a finished mountain pony or pack mule is seven to nine years. Figuring the cost of feed, pasture, vet bills, fencing, taxes... you're thinking about a $2,000 horse and there's no guarantee he'll even be alive at the end of that time, much less that he'll be what you want.

Bargains are so few and far between that it's probably best if you go horse or mule shopping prepared to pay the going price and intent on buying the best stock you can afford. Don't let us blind you to the possibility that the best horse is the horse you already own. This section has been primarily for people who either have no horses or who have to add to their string in order to start packing. If you already own saddle horses that are reliable and that you're comfortable with, pack them. Don't start trading around just because your critters don't look like Jiggs.

Training and Conditioning.

One way or another you now have a string of good, steady, broke horses, enough for everyone in the family to ride and a few extra to pack. You're finally ready to go to the mountains. Right? Wrong. First your animals have got to go to school, and for pack stock as with children, that means back to basics, including a certain amount of phys. ed.

If your horse or mule is barefoot, have him shod. Don't wait until the night before you leave. Newly shod horses are often tender footed at first, and if you ride them immediately into rocky country, they stay that way. A slightly high nail may not cause lameness for a few days, and if you leave immediately after shoeing, you may find yourself in the hills with a lame horse.

The best shoe is no shoe. The hoof functions best when it is free to expand as it strikes the ground. Also, shoeing contributes to dry, brittle hooves by puncturing the hoof with nails and removing its natural lacquer. Unfortunately the hoof isn't designed to withstand the

*Figure 11.
An experienced horse.
We don't recommend this,
but it illustrates
the disposition desirable
in mountain stock.*

Harley Hettick

abuse inflicted by hard rocky ground — remember, horses are a plains animal — so shoes are a necessary evil. For pleasure riding, the shoe which most clearly mimics the hoof's natural unshod condition is a flat plate. If the country you'll be traveling in is neither steep nor rocky and is free of snow and ice, a plate is the best shoe. However, over most of the West, you can't count on any of these conditions applying. A shoe with calks at both heel and toe is the most functional for packing and is what we use on our stock. In summer, the calks give added traction over rocks; in fall and winter when trails freeze and become snow covered, they are essential.

Fully calked shoes can cause injuries in horses asked to perform at speed. If you also use your saddle horses in performance events, replace his calked shoes with something more suitable following your pack trip.

We already mentioned the importance of living experience to a good mountain horse or pack mule. An animal doesn't accumulate that overnight, but you can help the process along by seeing that he's exposed to kids, dogs, trucks, chain saws, fire crackers... just about any sort of sudden excitement that might upset him.

We assume you've followed our advice and bought steady, older horses to pack or else you're going to pack one of your saddle horses. No matter how well-broke that horse is, unless he's packed before, you should give him a chance to learn to carry a dead weight on a pack saddle. Suddenly having packs swaying from either side of a pack saddle can upset even a calm horse. He's got to learn to balance on steep slopes without any help from a rider, and he's got to learn that with his load, he's wider. Trees that he'd fit between with you on his back might not be wide enough apart for him and his load, and on narrow trails he can't hug the face of the cliff. Unless you can afford to leave a lot of broken gear strewn about the mountains, you'd better give him a chance to learn these things close to home. Start him packing with a couple of bales. They're cheap, soft and unbreakable.

Most horses and some mules have an initial aversion to packing game. Because the necessary teaching props are rarely available at home, teaching stock to pack game is usually undertaken in the hills and memorable battles between packer and pack animal have resulted. You'll have the least trouble if you can introduce a new horse or mule gradually to packing game. Take the uneducated animal out to the game to be packed in the company of an experienced horse or mule. Pack the meat on the experienced animal and tie the green one behind where he can get used to the sight and smell. After going along as an extra one or two times, the horse may remain wary of game, but should let you load him with it. If he doesn't, you have to resort to the same quickie method available to the packer with only one horse or without any horse or mule broken to pack meat.

A horse's aversion to dead game animals seems to be a response to both the sight and the smell. The popular idea that horses are frightened by the smell of blood is, we feel,

Figure 12.
*A blindfold
improvised from
a denim jacket.*

a myth. Deer, elk, and bear each have distinctive odors that have nothing to do with blood. It seems likely that these are what a horse responds to. In any case, there is little you can do about the odor of game except give the pack horse or mule a chance to grow accustomed to it. If you follow some version of the following procedure, you should be able to load your game.

Lead the horse (everything that follows applies equally to mules) toward the game from a direction that lets him see and smell it from as far away as possible. You should be able to get fairly close. Then tie the horse to a stout tree. Tie him short — six inches isn't too short — and about chin high or a little higher. If the horse is ignoring the carcass, he may not have seen it. Move it. He'll notice.

Bring a small part of the carcass, such as a swatch of hide or even the head to him and let him smell it. He will snort and blow and may even try to strike at it. That's why you tied him short.

When he'll tolerate the smell, it's time to load. Mantying the meat (see Chapter four) can sometimes make this much easier since some horses will pay little more attention to mantied game than they do any other load. Blindfolding will have nearly the same effect, though there's a moment of truth when the blindfold comes off and the horse

looks back and sees what's on his back. A blindfold is easily improvised from a shirt or jacket by tucking the sleeves through the cheek pieces of the halter (Figure 12).

If the horse strikes at you as you load, tie up a hind foot. A simple, safe way of doing this is illustrated in Figures 13a through e. Tie a bowline (Appendix II) around the pack animal's neck with one end of about 30 feet of soft rope. If you think you might be kicked should you try to pick up a hind foot, stretch the rope out behind the horse. Stand well back and try to get him to step over the rope with one hind foot. Flicking the rope lightly against the fetlock will sometimes encourage him to lift a foot momentarily so you can get the rope under it. When you succeed, move forward to the shoulder, and pull on the end of the rope to raise the foot up toward the horse's belly. Work quickly and don't be afraid to get the foot high. The higher the foot, the harder it will be for him to struggle. Wrapping the rope two or three times around the pastern will lessen the chances of rope burns. Tie off the jerk-end of the rope to the loop of the bowline with a quick release knot (Figure 13e). Of course with an animal accustomed to having its feet handled, you can simply lift the foot, take a few turns around the pastern and tie off the end of the rope.

Not many horses will fight seriously with

a.

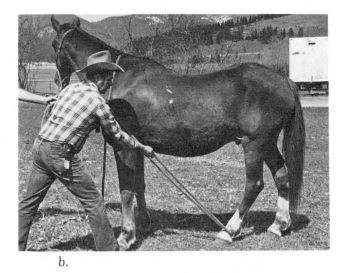

b.

c.

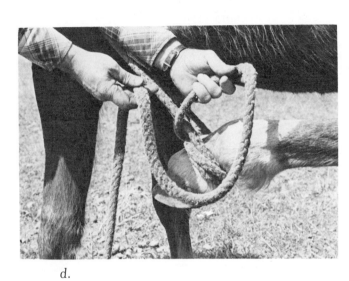

d.

Figure 13a-e.
Sequence
showing how
to tie up
a hind foot.
Notice the soft,
woven rope in d.

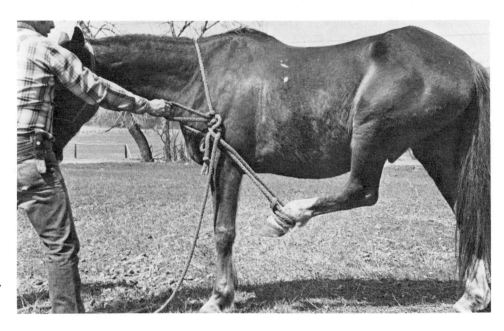

e.

a blindfold on and a leg tied up, and if you're on a slope, the footing will inhibit them even further. A horse that fights you under these conditions isn't the kind we've suggested for the hills. He's also likely to fall over. Don't panic if this happens. Take advantage of the fact that he's on the ground, and keep him there awhile to think things over. If you sit on his neck just behind his head and hold his muzzle in the air, he won't be able to get up. Because a horse is a prey animal who depends on his speed for defense, nothing makes an impression on him like depriving him of his feet, and the impression he'll get while you're holding him down is that resisting you is pointless. He'll be much deflated when you let him up.

It should be obvious that we're now discussing an extreme situation. We don't recommend that you throw an animal intentionally, just to load him with meat. Throwing a horse or mule is never without some risk even when you can select a soft, level surface. If you try to throw a horse in many of the places you're likely to have game down, you'll kill the horse or at best get to watch him roll to the bottom of the hill.

Once you have the game loaded (see Chapter four for a discussion of the proper hitches), leave the horse tied and remove the blindfold. Give him a few minutes to get used to the "thing" on his back. When you do untie him, don't lead him off right away. He may blow up when the load starts to rock. Freshly killed game can look — and probably feel — very alive when the load starts to rock. This is less of a problem if the meat has stiffened, is frozen, or is mantied. Keep a firm, short hold on the lead rope. Possibly the best thing that can happen now is for your horse to want to graze. Let him. Most horses would rather eat than fight, and the gentle movement of the load as he grazes will let him get accustomed to that meaty "thing" with legs, swaying on his back. If there is no grass or the horse is uninterested, start him off slowly and cautiously — a few steps at a time — until you see how he'll act. Hang on.

We don't want to discourage you from using your stock to pack game. (It sure beats packing it yourself.) We've merely tried to prepare you for the range of problems you can encounter the first time you try it with an uninitiated horse. It's important to remember that having an animal, dead or otherwise, on his back arouses a horse's most deeply rooted instincts for self-preservation. If you've bought the type of pack horse we recommend, if you take your time and don't get mad, there's an excellent chance you'll load your horse with no more resistance than some histrionic snorting.

Another thing your pack stock must learn is to trail quietly behind one another without racing or hanging back. Teaching a green horse or mule not to hang back is usually a matter of practice. He'll learn to pace himself to your string after being pulled along for awhile, but if he's your only pack horse, pulling him for 20 miles through the hills can be hard on you. Again, teach him at home. Mules, even good ones,

*Figure 14.
A half-hitch
across a mule's nose
will quickly convince her
that keeping up
is in her best interests.*

will sometimes start hanging back when loaded. Looping the lead rope across her nose (Figure 14) will quickly convince a recalcitrant mule that keeping pace is the smart thing to do. There are specially made "come along" halters available which have a similar effect. An mule who starts hanging back may only need such a convincer occasionally to help her see the error of her ways. For some, however, the arrangement has to become permanent. Horses sometimes need this treatment, too. But once is usually enough.

A horse that tries to charge past the horse ahead can be more of a problem. Usually the problem is excess energy, and a few days on the trail under 180 pounds of food will convince even the most rambunctious character that he's not in a race. In the meantime, we recommend having one rider lead him while another comes along behind and holds him back with a second, longer lead rope. In a pack string of several horses, a charger can be restrained by running his lead rope through a loop around the back pad of the horse in front of him (see Figure 15). Avoid swatting him in the face with your hat or a lead rope when he tries to come past. At best you'll make him head shy. At worst he'll learn to circle around you out of reach at the end of his lead rope,

and you and your saddle horse will find yourselves jaw to jaw with the pack horse who's supposed to be behind you. Some saddle horses — like my own mare — will solve this problem for you. They dislike being passed and will greet an overly enthusiastic mule with flattened ears and gnashing teeth. This is horse language, and the message "stay in line" is unmistakable.

Unless he's been packed before or used in rugged country, your budding pack horse may not pay enough attention to where his feet are going. Even some mules will lack the surefootedness and agility typical of their kind. A pack animal doesn't see much in front of him except the back end of the animal ahead. Obstacles appear suddenly, and he has to see them and handle them without hesitating. Lead him through rough country, over logs, through rocks or even over bales of hay. If he still won't watch his feet, put a tiedown on him in these obstacle courses. But don't use one in the hills; there he needs his neck free for balance.

Any horse or mule going into the mountains has got to stand quietly when tied, both alone and with other horses. Pawers and diggers can be hard on horseshoes to say nothing of grass and trees. Some horses can dig such deep holes overnight that you practically need a winch to get them out in the morning. The Forest Service and other agencies and landowners take a dim view of such destruction, and too much of it can only lead to restrictions on horse use. We don't want to see that. If your horse paws when he's tied, hobble him a few times. You can use the same cure for horses that paw and kick in the truck or trailer. One or two trips with the hobbles on will break that habit.

Get both your saddle horse and pack stock used to the extra gear you'll be carrying and using on the trail. Raincoats being put on probably cause more wrecks in the mountains than anything else. Just taking off a hat can unsettle a horse unused to seeing a rider's hands anywhere but behind his neck. With his eyes set out there on the sides, a horse has a pretty good view of you and what you're doing. Move around a lot in the saddle. Take things out of your saddle bags. If you're going to take pictures from the saddle, get him used to the sound of the shutter. The whir of a movie camera can start a rodeo. Make sure you can get on or off either side. Start this by dismounting on the off side a few times. If your horse objects or shies, you stand a good chance of landing on your feet. Once he's used to this, start mounting on the off side. Being able to do this is not only a convenience on narrow, side-hill trails, it can save your life in an emergency.

Finally, get him used to all sorts of terrain. A pack animal has got to learn not to rush streams, boggy trails or steep hills. Yours might think a hill is only fifty yards long because that's how far it is to the end of the rise he sees. You know it's five miles to the top.

At the same time you're training your stock, you can be conditioning them. Too many people take unridden, butterball

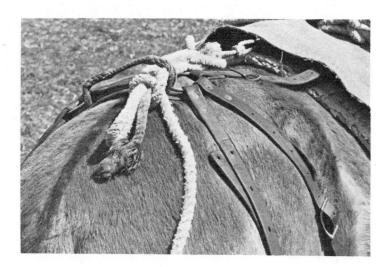

Figure 15.
Lacing his
lead rope through
a loop on the backpad
of the horse ahead
will help keep
an over eager
pack animal in line.

20

horses out of their pasture, load them into the trailer and then go into the mountains. If you do that to your fatso, he'll probably make it, but you'll be shortening his useful life.

You don't have to spend months getting your animals ready for a one-week pack trip, particularly if they live outdoors. Two weeks before your planned trip is plenty of lead time, and even then you don't have to work the horse every day. Six rides will do it. We recommend four two-hour rides with loads (use hay bales) over varied terrain and easy obstacles and two longer rides of about four hours each, including some hard conditioning on steep hills. Try to do a little of everything on each ride. Tie your horse. Use your camera. Put on and take off a raincoat. Get on and off both sides.

These rides will be good for you, too. You'll enjoy your pack trip more if you're not unbearably saddle sore the first few days.

USFS

Figure 17a. A sawbuck.

Figure 17b. A Decker.

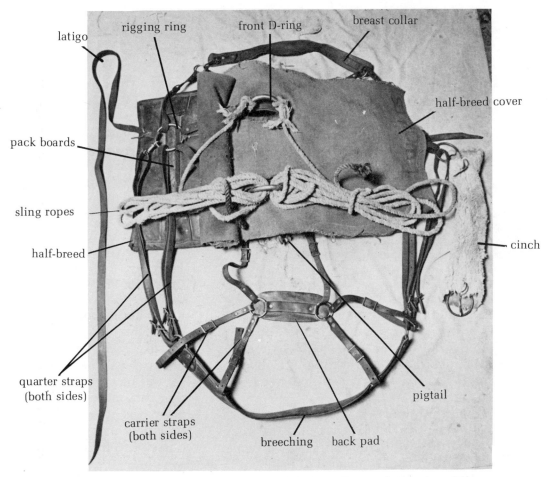

latigo — rigging ring — front D-ring — breast collar — half-breed cover — pack boards — sling ropes — half-breed — cinch — quarter straps (both sides) — carrier straps (both sides) — breeching — back pad — pigtail

Figure 18. *Parts of a pack saddle.*

chapter three
Deckers & Sawbucks

To pack you need a pack saddle. Practically, your choices are limited to the Decker and the sawbuck, the only two pack saddles in widespread use today. There have been others — the Phillips, the aparejo, the McClellan; even stock saddles will serve, but of these, the first two are now little more than historical curiosities; the last two are expedients.

The sawbuck has ancient origins. Its design is simple and variations, such as the camel saddle of the Middle East, appear world wide. As the pack saddle of the fur trapper and the prospector, the sawbuck played a role in opening the American west. In the years following the Lewis and Clark expedition, sawbucks packed just about everything a horse could carry.

If the sawbuck is an institution, the Decker is an upstart. It seems likely that the Decker idea originated from a west-coast packer known as "Old Man McDaniel." The modern Decker saddle was perfected by O.P. Robinett of Kooskia, Idaho shortly after 1906. Originally known as the O.P.R. after its maker, the Decker finally took its name from the Decker Brothers, packers from the same region, who began making the saddle around 1930 under an agreement with Robinett. At that time — the twilight of the old west — a generation of packers skilled in the use of the sawbuck and the traditional diamond hitch were passing into history, while a rapidly growing Forest Service needed transport for heavy, often bulky equipment through the vast unroaded

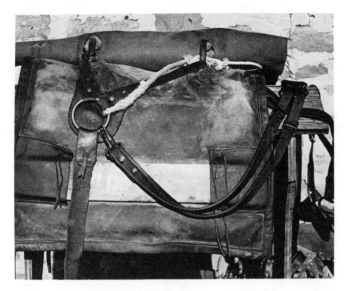

Figure 19a-b.
The saddle on the left is
rigged in the "full-rigged"
position, directly below the
front D-ring. The saddle on
the right is rigged slightly
behind "center-fire." A full
range of intermediate
positions is possible.

back-country. The Decker, a rugged, versatile saddle that could be easily packed to capacity by Forest Service personnel, filled this need. It caught on quickly throughout Idaho, Montana, Oregon and Washington, while in Wyoming, Colorado, and California packers continue to use the sawbuck.

Figure 18 shows the harness and parts of a Decker. A sawbuck is basically the same but with these differences — a sawbuck has wooden crossbucks instead of metal D-rings and lacks the half-breed and half-breed cover. Also the sawbuck is typically double-rigged (two cinches). There are, however, less obvious differences that give each saddle distinct characteristics, and you should take these into consideration when selecting a pack saddle.

The Decker is substantially stronger than the sawbuck. This is due almost entirely to the metal D-rings. The bucks of a sawbuck are more fragile, and if a mule falls or rolls on them, they usually break. D-rings will occasionally bend, but will rarely break. Even so, you check the fit of a Decker carefully after an accident and rebend D-rings to their original position. A cocked tree will work on a pack animal's back and sore him.

The Decker can also be fitted to any horse or mule. D-rings can be bent to make the tree wider or narrower, and the bars of the tree can be rasped to better conform to the curve of the back. The configuration of a sawbuck tree can be altered only slightly without dismantling the whole saddle and

replacing or remounting the crossbucks. Because the bars of a sawbuck tend to be thinner and shorter than those on a Decker, the degree to which they can be shaped is limited. Many older sawbucks were built for burrows. These have very short bars and should never be used on a horse. Loaded, they rock more than a longer saddle and can gouge the horse's back front and rear. With its longer bars, the proper sawbuck for horses and mules is the "humane" sawbuck.

A third adjustment permitted by the Decker but not the sawbuck is rigging position. The range of rigging positions is shown in Figure 19. Rigging position, because it controls the location of the girth on the horse, is critical in avoiding girth sores. The rigging of a Decker buckles to the tree beneath the half-breed and is easily adjustable over a wide range. The rigging of a sawbuck is screwed or riveted to the tree and can't be changed without major surgery.

The sawbuck is typically "double rigged" — it has two girths to the Decker's one. Some packers cite this as an advantage for the sawbuck since it stabilizes the load and better distributes the friction around the mule's middle. Few sawbuck users fully realize this advantage, however, since many animals tend to become a little bronky when a girth is tightened around their stomach. The second girth also adds to saddling time and if too tight, may impede a mule's breathing.

We believe that better fit and greater strength make the Decker a more versatile

b.

saddle than the sawbuck. The same animal can carry heavier loads under a Decker because the weight is better distributed, and the saddle itself holds up better. The Decker is designed to be loaded with two equal loads, packaged in canvas sheets called manties, instead of the panyards and diamond-hitched top-load typically used with a sawbuck. The use of mantied loads gives still greater versatility to the Decker. This will become clearer in chapter five. Admittedly, the differences in the way each saddle is loaded reflect tradition more than any intrinsic characteristic of either saddle. Both Deckers and sawbucks can be loaded with either manties or panyards. Besides overall strength, the only structural difference making Deckers more suited to mantied loads than sawbucks is the half-breed with its pack boards. Pack boards distribute the weight of a mantied load more widely along a horse's or mule's ribs. If you're a sawbuck owner who wants to pack with mantied loads, you should consider fitting your saddle with a half-breed and pack boards.

The price of the Decker's greater strength is greater weight. A fully rigged Decker typically weighs 25 pounds while a sawbuck weighs only 16 to 18 pounds. Since the weight of the saddle is part of your pack animal's total load, the difference is weight that doesn't go as gear.

Another real advantage of the sawbuck is good availability. Though there are only a few active sawbuck makers, there are simply more sawbucks in use, and used sawbucks are not hard to find. A new, good quality sawbuck sells for about $125, but if that's beyond your means, sawbucks are easily made in a home woodshop. Deckers are harder to obtain. Because they are a recent innovation and in demand, few used Deckers are available. Occasionally one can be purchased in an auction, second-hand store, or pawn shop, but good Deckers from these sources are rare. There are a few saddlemakers specializing in Deckers, and you may be able to talk a local riding saddle maker into producing some for you. Expect to pay between $200 and $250 for a quality Decker.[1] Anything less than this and you can be almost sure that corners were cut, and the saddle is inferior.

Both pack saddles are simple enough that only a few items determine quality. The bars of the tree should be softwood and should fit your horse's back without gouging or excessive rocking. Remember that these can be shaped somewhat for a better fit. The bucks of a sawbuck should be hardwood. D-rings on a Decker can be either steel or brass (steel is easier to adjust), and should be attached with bolts or rivets that can be tightened. Leather fittings should be of quality heavy harness leather.

Don't be intimidated by the task of judging leather. Leather quality is most often the difference between a good saddle and a cheap saddle. Good leather will feel good. It will be supple, smooth and heavy, and it will have a uniform thickness. Avoid

[1]The price of leather has risen astronomically in recent years. If the trend continues, these figures will rapidly be out of date.

thin, dry leather, or leather that creases or cracks when you fold it. Dye and metal studs are often used to cover defects; good leather doesn't need to be dressed up. Trust your impulse. If it feels good to you, it probably is. We should mention, though, that nearly all leather these days is impregnated with wax which gives it a nice smooth feel, protects it and, not incidentally, adds weight, making it more expensive.

Inexpensive Deckers and sawbucks sometimes substitute canvas, neoprene or nylon for leather. We believe leather harness is superior to any of these. Well dressed leather offers a combination of durability and flexibility under all conditions and temperatures that these substitutes can't match. Also, leather, because it retains some of the characteristics of living skin, is one of the few materials that's compatible over long periods with the moving, sweating hide of a mule or horse. If you doubt this, consider why plastic shoes have never caught on among humans.

Fitting Pack Saddles

Pack saddles should be individually fitted to a particular pack animal by first stripping the saddle to the tree and putting it on without a pad. The job is easier if the horse or mule has shed his winter coat. If necessary, use a wood rasp to shape the ends of the bars so they don't gouge the horse. The bars should turn up slightly front and back so when the loaded saddle rocks, it won't dig into the horse. Carefully bend the D-rings of a Decker so the bars lie flat against the animal's back without pinching. Heating the D-rings with a propane torch will make them easier to bend, but don't burn the tree. Be particularly careful bending brass D-rings; they have a tendency to bend unevenly. Depending on how the crossbucks are linked, it may be possible to change the fork angle of a sawbuck slightly. Once the tree is fitted, you can reassemble and adjust the harness.

Most people unthinkingly use the cinch that comes with their saddle. If it seems too long, they shorten it up on the off side; too short and they lengthen it. Don't do this to your horse. The cinch rings on the girth should fit just below the lateral blood vessel along the horse's flank and slightly behind and above the elbow. An old timer in Missoula who has saddled a lot of horses says the cinch ring should go "half a ring behind the elbow and half a ring above the point of the elbow." That's a good rule of thumb. Measure your horse and buy a cinch that will put the cinch ring the right distance up the horse's side.

The right cinch length doesn't insure that your cinch will be properly positioned; the rigging position must be right or the girth

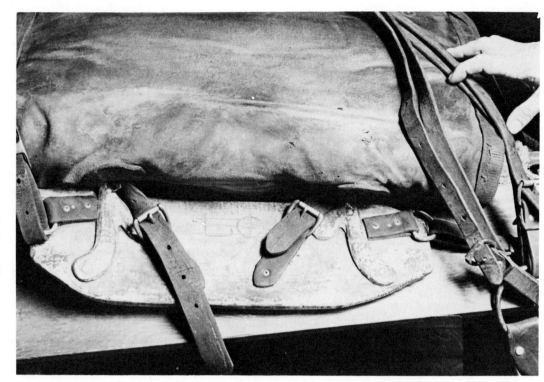

Figure 20.
Buckles on the
Decker tree
permit a full
range of rigging
position adjustments.

will be too far back. The only way to change the rigging on a sawbuck is to take out the rivets holding it and rerivet it in a different location. This is drastic, but it can be done. Moving the saddle forward or back might avoid girth sores but only at the expense of sore shoulders or a sore back. Don't do it. The rigging on a Decker buckles to the tree at the base of each D-ring. By tightening at one buckle and loosening at the other, you can adjust your Decker over the full range of rigging positions from full to center fire. If in doubt about a rigging position, remember that no harm will be done if you rig a little behind the optimal position, as long as the girth crosses the animal's brisket and doesn't encircle the belly where it will interfere with breathing. Rigged too far forward, a cinch can rub an open sore in as little as half a mile.

Many people buy Deckers and put them into service without knowing this adjustment is possible. Late one fall when Smoke was returning from his hunting camp in the Bitterroot Mountains, he noticed occasional drops of blood in the snow on the trail. A mile or two later he saw a rider ahead leading a pack horse that was obviously in pain; the horse flinched with each step and was moving very slowly. As Smoke got closer he could see that the rider knew how to pack. His loads were tight and well balanced. Everything except the pack horse was as it should be.

When he caught up, Smoke saw that the cinch rings had rubbed open sores on the pack horse's sides. The young rider told Smoke that the saddle was new and it didn't seem to fit. The saddle was obviously rigged too far forward so Smoke showed the fellow how it adjusted. They were able to adjust it backwards so that his mare could walk out of the mountains without further aggravating her wounds. Even though the young man was a fairly accomplished packer, he had no idea the rigging of his Decker was adjustable.

The critical piece of harness on a pack saddle is the breeching (pronounced "britchen"). To position it, first adjust the back straps so the back pad is halfway between the croup and the point of the hip.

Next, adjust the carrier straps so that the breeching hangs four inches below the curve of the haunch and parallel to the ground. Quarter straps should just be slack when the animal is standing normally. If your saddle has two quarter straps on each side — and it should — the bottom one should be slightly looser than the top.

Figure 21 shows a properly adjusted breeching. The horse can stride out without being hindered, yet the breeching is tight enough to keep the saddle from sliding more than two inches forward. Some very conscientious packers will stop before a long, steep downhill and tighten the quarter straps on all their saddles. At the bottom these are loosened again.

Similarly, you should check the breeching adjustment of a saddle each spring even when it is used on the same animal as the previous fall. Some packers have problems with breeching soring their stock the first trip each year. This is often because their pack horse or mule has gained weight while standing around all winter and spring, and the breeching adjustment that was right in the fall is now too tight. You may have to let quarter straps out a notch or two in the spring, then take them in as the season goes along.

The breast collar is not nearly as important as most people imagine, yet it can cause problems. A pack animal should be able to get his head down to drink easily with the breast collar on. Too high or too tight and the collar can restrict breathing on steep upgrades. A tight cinch around an animal's narrowest circumference does more to keep the saddle from sliding back than a properly adjusted breast collar, particularly if he has a bit of a hay belly. Regard the breast collar as insurance

Figure 21.
Properly
adjusted
breeching.

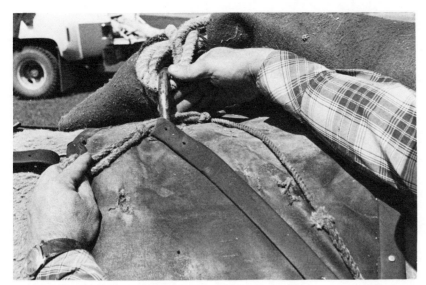

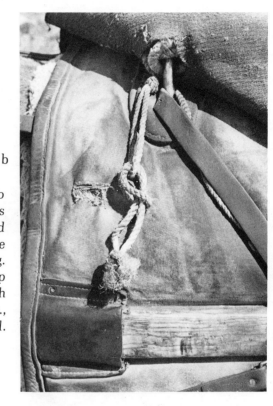

Figure 22a-b.
Pigtail attachment:
a. a loop of
unbreakable quarter-inch
nylon rope is

a

b

eye-spliced to
the rigging rings
and extended
through the
rear D-ring.
A six-inch loop
of quarter-inch
manila, b.,
is then attached.

against a loose girth.

Pack saddles come from the maker equipped with half-breed, cinches, breeching and breast collar. The half-breed, which is simply a canvas envelope, may or may not be stuffed. If it isn't, you will have to fill it. Deer hair, horse hair, or even dried bear grass make acceptable half-breed stuffing. Many Decker makers use rubberized pig hair. This provides excellent cushioning and is very durable. An upholstery supply dealer can order it for you. The half-breed should be filled to a uniform one- to two-inch thickness. Continuous abrasion from swaying packs will eventually wear out a half-breed. You can prolong the life of yours by adding a half-breed cover to your saddle. This is simply a piece of rugged fabric cut to the dimensions of the half-breed and slotted to fit over the D-rings. Drier's felt, if you can get it, makes excellent half-breed covers.

You will also have to add your own pigtail and sling ropes. A pigtail is a loop of low-tensil-strength rope used to tie in lead ropes when linking mules into a string. If a mule falls or gets into trouble, she will break free rather than endangering the entire string. Figure 22 shows how the pigtail is eye-spliced to both rigging rings with a loop feeding out through the rear D-ring. Some packers make their pigtails entirely out of breakable rope, but each time one of these breaks, it has to be repaired or replaced. This is a nuisance on the trail. It is cheaper and easier to use something

unbreakable like quarter-inch nylon as a permanent pigtail. Breakable loops four to six inches long are looped into this. These are quickly replaced from a supply carried in your saddlebags. Use inexpensive quarter-inch manila or hemp for your breakaway loops. These are strong enough to pull along a recalcitrant mule but will break when they have to. With anything smaller, mules and horses learn that they can break loose whenever they decide you're going too fast or the hill is too steep.

For sling ropes, we recommend 33 feet of one-half inch diameter spun (soft-twist) nylon, eye-spliced at one end and back-spliced on the other (see Appendix II). Twenty-two to 24 feet is adequate, but the extra length is available as an emergency rope supply. Use the eye splice to loop the sling ropes to the front D-ring. Lace the ropes for the basket hitch (chapter four) and

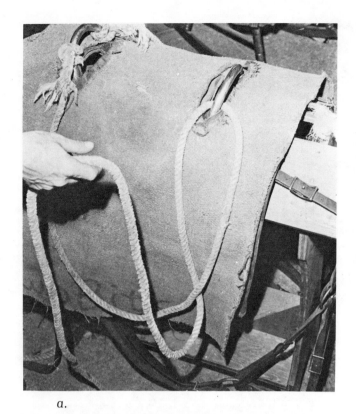

a.

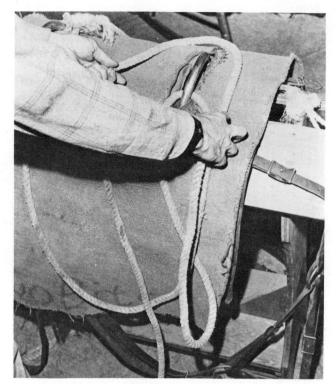

b.

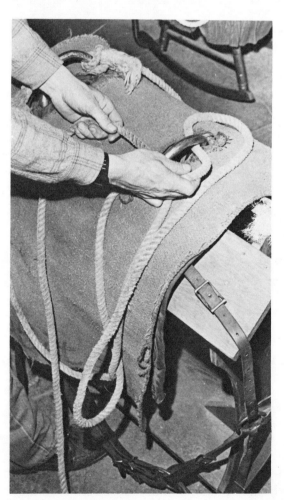

c.

Figure 23a-f.
Sequence showing
how to store
sling ropes
on a Decker.

put up the slack on the rear D-ring as in Figure 23a-f.

To put up the rigging of a Decker when not in use, place the back pad and the breeching neatly on the saddle between the D-rings. Flip the girth up from the off-side, thread the breast collar through the front D-ring, through the cinch ring on the girth, over the back pad and breeching and out the rear D-ring. The latigo can simply be draped across the top of the saddle. Stored this way, the saddle can be easily carried and swung onto an animal's back. When the saddle is completely rigged and fitted to a particular animal, label it with that animal's name on either the half-breed or the half-breed cover.

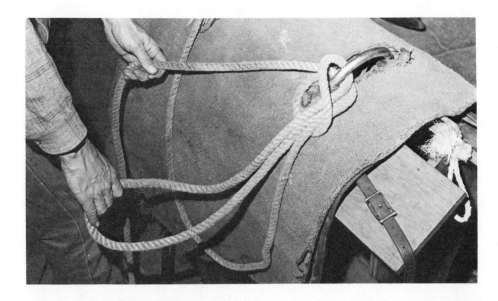

d.

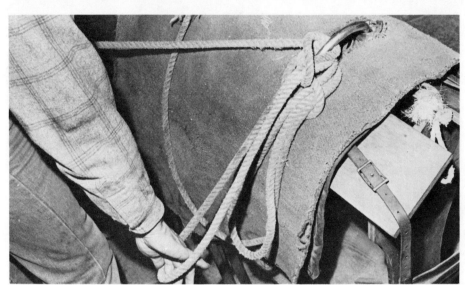

e.

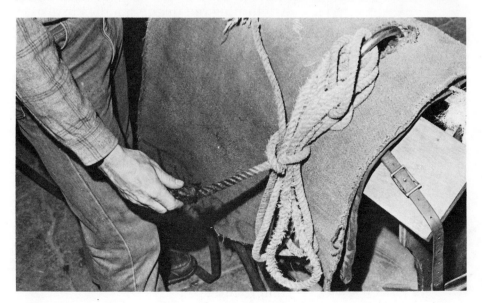

f.

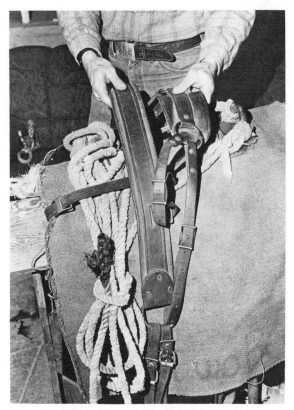

a.

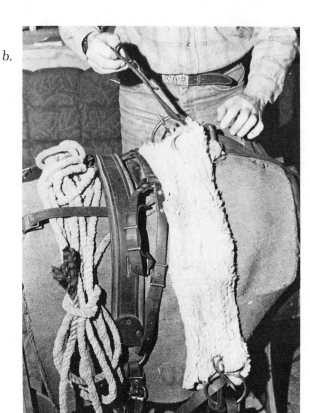

b.

Figure 24a-c.
Putting up a Decker when not in use.

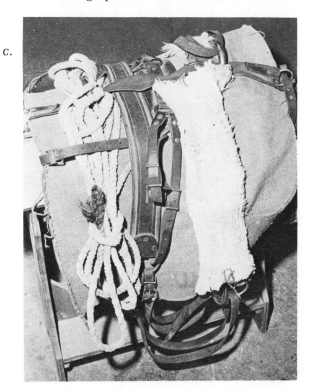

c.

Riding Saddles for the Mountains

Riding saddles come in endless variations. At the turn of the century, every cowtown in the west had a saddle maker or two turning out quality saddles in a style each felt was best. These men knew their business, and even today the most economical saddle suitable for mountain travel is an older saddle that has been well maintained.

There is no one perfect type of saddle for the mountains, and most western stock saddles are quite serviceable. You probably already have a saddle, and we hardly expect you·to rush out and trade it in on one that more closely approximates our idea of a good mountain saddle. Few people use their horses or their saddles exclusively for a single type of riding, so even if you buy a new saddle or have one made for you, your saddle is going to represent a degree of compromise.

Figure 25. Several saddles that have been used successfully in the mountains. No one is perfect. Look at each carefully and appraise how closely it approaches the "ideal" mountain saddle described in the text.

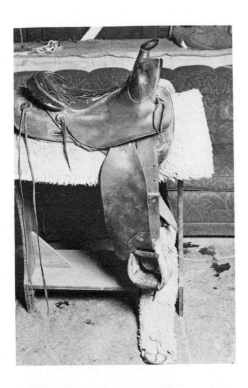

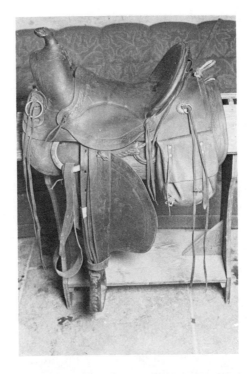

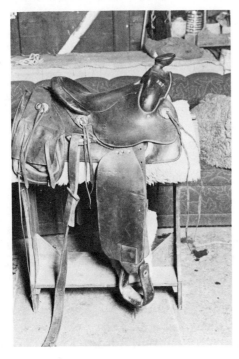

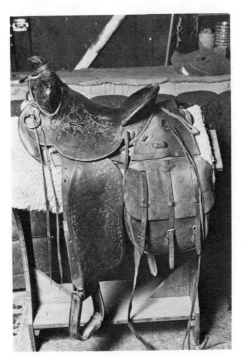

There are certain characteristics that affect a saddle's suitability for sustained backcountry use. The most important is that the rigging be right for your horse. Riggings on riding saddles aren't adjustable, but with only a little effort, you should be able to find what you need. If you special order a saddle, you can specify rigging position. At least 90 percent of the stock saddles in saddle shops come full-rigged. These work well for ranch and arena work, but in the hills they may cause girth sores on horses with poor withers or straight-up shoulders. A rigging closer to seven-eighths or three-quarters is better for daily use in the mountains. These can be somewhat harder to find.

Next, the tree must be long enough to distribute your weight on the horse's back. The heavier you are, the more important this is. A longer tree also relieves some of the pressure on a horse's loins from overloaded saddle bags. The tree should extend three to five inches beyond the back of the cantle.

Tree fork configuration should be important, but this is a feature over which most riders have little control. Nearly all heavier stock saddles are built on a semi-quarter horse tree, six and a quarter to seven and a half inches wide at the base of the fork and about seven and three-quarters inches high in the gullet. Some lighter saddles, usually designed for barrel racing, are built on a higher, narrower tree: otherwise anything but the quarter horse tree requires a special order with a minimum wait of three months.

Fortunately, the quarter-horse tree will fit most western-type horses, and can be used on even high-withered horses by adding an extra saddle pad.

Finally, the saddle has to fit you. You've got to be comfortable in it all day long, uphill and down. For downhill riding a saddle needs some swells, but these needn't be extreme. Swells between nine and 12 inches across are adequate. The seat, available in lengths from 13 to 17 inches, should be long enough to fit you comfortably. Many people buy their saddles too big. Sit in a lot of different saddles, and you'll learn what feels good. You also want a fairly flat seat and high cantle. The high cantle provides lower-back support and encourages you to sit up and ride properly over your horse's center of gravity. Most recreational riders have a tendency to slouch after a few hours in the saddle. This is hard on you and your horse. A high cantle provides a constant, gentle reminder to sit erect.

Many modern stock saddles are built, unfortunately, with an extreme slope to the rear and a low cantle. This is a specialty configuration for competitive roping where it is an aid in fast stops and quick dismounts. In the 1950's and into the 60's, most factory saddles were built on this design. Recently the situation has improved and flatter, deeper seats are again readily available.

Smooth, rather than rough-out leather, long jockey flaps, and free swinging stirrups can all add to comfort over a long day's riding. Both of us find padded seats

Figure 26.
Martingale style
breast collar.

Other Tack

Most riders in mountainous country like to use a breast collar. We recommend the style in Figure 26 since it directs the pressure against the horse's shoulders where it won't hinder breathing or drinking. The best breast collars are made of double thickness leather, latigo inside the saddle leather outside. Girth style breast collars are cheaper and cooler, but they tend to pick up burs and debris. Fur-covered collars have the same defect.

Croupers, usually seen only on harness horses, are so useful that it's surprising more riders don't use them. If you ride a low-withered mule, a crouper is essential. By holding the saddle back on downgrades a crouper allows the use of a looser girth. Horses quickly become used to a crouper under their tail and will learn to take hold of it by tucking their tails down tightly to hold the saddle back.

uncomfortable, but most saddles these days come padded so we are out of the mainstream. Suit yourself. Similarly, wide stirrups with three or four inch treads enjoy great popularity. We prefer two inch treads because they're easier to keep free of mud and ice, and they're safer when used with vibram-soled pacs in winter. The narrower tread is only less comfortable if you ride in cheap, soft-soled riding boots or shoes.

Finally, the saddle horn should be substantial enough to anchor a rope in case a mule gets stuck in the mud or goes down a steep bank. Otherwise it's irrelevant except as a handle for mounting. Also irrelevant is the flank cinch on double-rigged saddles. The only function of a flank cinch in the mountains is to snag brush and branches. We suggest you take it off. The one exception occurs when a full-double rigged saddle, used without a flank cinch, rubs a sore. Then a snug flank cinch may keep the front cinch back in a non-irritating position.

Figure 27. A crouper. To use one you may have to have a ring attached behind the cantle. A crouper, like this one, with buckles on either side of the tail is easier to use.

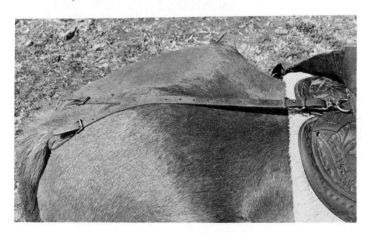

Figure 28. *A good synthetic fleece pad.*

Saddle bags are so useful they encourage more-is-better thinking. Saddle bags should be small — a good size is ten inches by ten inches by three inches. That's large enough for lunch, a camera and binoculars. Your other gear belongs on a pack horse.

The problem with large saddle bags is that you will fill them — a variation on Murphy's Law — and they put the weight on the wrong part of the horse. If you must tie heavy items to your riding saddle, put them in front of you. We've made the point before, but it's so important it bears repeating — horses and mules that are loaded heavily behind the saddle develop sore backs and ultimately spinal arthritis.

Several equipment manufacturers have come out with what we think is the ultimate in saddlebag foolishness: large nylon saddlebags with a third compartment behind the saddle to hold a sleeping bag and extra clothes. The idea is to permit people to go light for a weekend without a pack horse. We have experimented with several of these, all of which work but could be better designed. All are too big. People using these bags will overfill them and horses are going to be injured.

A single pad, if it's a good one, is all you need for mountain riding and packing unless a saddle fits poorly. A good saddle pad should be big enough to allow at least two inches all around the saddle. It must be resiliant enough and thick enough to provide padding, yet breathable and absorbant to allow air circulation and prevent sweat from accumulating. It should also be washable. If it is slick or slippery, you'll have a terrible time keeping it in place. Once a pad begins to slip the only way to get it back in place is to remove the loads and resaddle.

No pad is perfect, but measured against these criteria wool navajo-style blankets and artificial sheep-skin pads, like the "cool back" are excellent. Foam pads have serious deficiencies and thick hair pads are terrible.

Halters used in the hills should be strong. This is one of the few times that synthetics like nylon are superior to leather. Most leather show halters are too weak. If a leather halter is strong enough, it's too heavy; a horse has to carry it all day. We prefer flat, nylon halters because they are light, strong and fit well. The flat surface doesn't wear a groove in the horse's nose as round nylon and polypro do. Choose a halter that is easy to put on. Catching and haltering several snorty horses can be frustrating enough without fighting tight buckles and frozen knots.

Most packers leave the halter on, with lead rope attached, under their horse's bridle. The lead rope can be coiled and tied into the saddle strings, but a more convenient method employs a two-inch steel ring laced between the saddlestrings and concho. Figure 29a-d shows how the rope is put up so that it can be retrieved simply and quickly by pulling the loose end.

Lead ropes should be 10 to 12 feet long and thick enough to afford a solid, comfortable grip. One-half inch diameter is a minimum. Commercially available lead ropes come with metal snaps. If you use these, buy good quality, heavy snaps. Because even good snaps sometimes break and ice up, we suggest that you make your

a.

Figure 29a-d. Putting up a lead rope using a ring on the saddle.
d. is an alternate method for long ropes; a loop is pulled through the ring and tied.

b.

c.

d.

own lead ropes omitting snaps entirely. Eye-splice one end and back-splice the other. You can eye splice directly to the halter ring, but by simply lassoing the halter ring, you keep the lead rope removable for other uses.

Saddle Care

There are schools of horsemanship that insist tack should be cleaned and saddle soaped after every use. This is nonsense. The idea probably arose when riding was the prerogative of the landed gentry, and no stable was complete without a groom or two to insure that milord's priviledged bottom was never sullied by a dirty saddle. Few of us have grooms and even fewer have the time or inclination to clean tack weekly or even monthly.

Good quality western tack is extremely durable; we are going to brave the purists'

outrage and say that one or two thorough cleanings a year is plenty. Late winter or early spring is a good time for the most extensive overhaul. By then a few unseasonably warm days can stir the urge to ride into the mountains, and a few bad days will have you wondering how all that snow can possibly be melted by the middle of June. Sitting down to clean tack is a good aid to pleasurable anticipation.

We suggest you begin by cleaning all leather parts of your saddles, bridles and harness (except latigos) with glycerin saddle soap. Use a sponge and work up a good thick lather. Lather the leather completely, then with the sponge wrung as dry as possible — but not rinsed — rub the lather into the leather rather than simply rinsing it off. Finish by oiling the saddle completely — both inner and outer surfaces. Smoke likes castor oil for this job because it deters rodents from chewing on leather. Castor oil is expensive, $15 to $20 a gallon and hard to find in quantity. A good drug store should be able to order it for you. If you can't find castor oil, neatsfoot oil — not neatsfoot compound — is the best substitute. Neatsfoot compounds rot stitching. Unless it's been oiled by the maker or your saddle shop, new leather will soak up a lot of oil. The oil softens the leather and protects it against the extremes of wetting and drying. You can overdo oiling, however. Once a year is plenty.

Latigos should get special treatment. We use nothing on ours but ordinary castile soap. Never oil a latigo; it will stretch and stretch and stretch...

While you've got the castille soap out, wash the fleece linings of your riding saddle skirts. Scrub them well with a stiff brush. If the fleeces are worn thin, you may want to take the saddle to a saddle shop and have them replaced. New fleeces are increasingly expensive and a good pad can make up for thin fleeces. A good saddlemaker can also flatten badly curled skirts in a press, but you can do this yourself. Remove the skirts (held on by the saddle strings and several light nails), and soak them overnight. Then lay them in the driveway between two pieces of plywood and park your car on them.

In the course of cleaning, you should examine every piece carefully for signs of wear or rot. By replacing questionable items, you can greatly reduce the chances of equipment failure in the hills. Half-breeds frequently need new or additional stuffing.

If you do one complete overhaul each winter, you need only do routine maintenance during the summer riding season. Try to keep your tack as dry as possible. Clean off the mud and dried sweat after every trip, using glycerin soap if you need to. Stirrup leathers, latigos and cinches are the most vulnerable parts of the saddle because they are soaked with sweat all day, each day the saddle is used. If you do a lot of riding, frequent saddle soaping during the summer is a good idea. In contrast to oiling, you can't saddle soap too often. Keep your girths and saddle pads clean. Wash them as often as necessary to keep them soft, absorbent and resilient.

With proper care, your tack can give you a lifetime of service. This involves some work, but if you buy quality equipment and appreciate the feel of good leather, it can be a labor of love. Well cared-for leather matures. There is no hurry-up way to give rich color, and fragrance that only come from use, from the wind and rain and sun working on leather that has been well soaped and oiled many times.

Figure 29a-b. *Two ways to package gear:*
a. a mule loaded with panyards;
b. two mules packing mantied loads.
Harley Hettick

a.

b.

chapter four
How To Pack A Cannonball

Making up loads and hanging them on a horse or mule is what packing is all about. Master packers can successfully pack just about anything a horse or a mule can carry: lumber, nail kegs, fence posts, hot water heaters. Smoke once packed an upright piano, and at the end of this chapter we'll tell you how he did it. Solving such unusual packing problems takes years of experience and a fertile imagination, but whether the items you pack are unusual or routine, the object is to attach them to a pack saddle so that they stay on the horse or mule without hurting him. A little theory, a few proven techniques and good sense are all you need to do this with almost anything that you're likely to take into the hills.

As a recreational packer, you're going to want to take sleeping bags, clothes, food, shelter, cooking gear and probably some grain and salt for your stock. To the problem of carrying such a wide array of unmatched items on each pack horse there are only two popular solutions: put everything in a pair of containers and hang these from the pack saddle, or wrap everything in a pair of packages and tie on the packages. In this country, containers are known as "panyards" which is Montanan for panniers. You may also hear them called alforjas or simply pack boxes. Packages of gear are known as manties (also spelled mantees or mantis) from the Spanish word *manta*, which means horse blanket. Confusing things even further, manty also refers to the canvas sheets in which a load is wrapped.

Panyards

Panyards are usually boxes or sacks with straps or hooks for attaching them to a pack saddle. Typical panyards will be 22 to 24 inches wide, 19 inches high and 10 to 12 inches thick, but the variety is almost endless since packers often make their own. Panyards have been made out of wood, plastic, fiber-glassed cardboard, and old steel drums, but the best panyards and the type we recommend that you use, if you decide to use panyards at all, are heavy canvas, reinforced with leather.

We're going to repeat our pitch for time-tested, natural materials, like leather or canvas for anything that you're going to put in contact with a horse's hide. Unyielding, impermeable materials and breathing, sweating horse-flesh aren't very compatible. Even if hard panyards are contoured to fit your horse or mule well (which is unlikely since hard panyards are often mass produced and horses aren't), they aren't worth it. Many packers say they like hard panyards to protect fragile items. Great. Your mule slips off the trail or pulls back and goes over. Your 79-cent-a-dozen eggs come through unscathed and so does your 16-dollar lantern. But your 1,000-dollar mule has a cracked rib, and you've got one animal's load to get out of the mountains in a splintered, dented or shattered panyard.

Panyards are undeniably easy to use, and for this reason they are used by most amateur packers as well as many professionals. Loading them properly is a simple matter of keeping hard, lumpy items away from your mule's sides, balancing each pair of panyards within five or six pounds of each other, buckling them to the D-rings of the Decker and heading down the trail. The only part that is at all tricky is balancing, and it's important. Pack both panyards at the same time. If you put a can of beans in one, put a can of peaches in the other. When you're done, heft each load to see how close they are. Then check your guess on the bathroom scale. Panyards have to be closely balanced because they allow for little adjustment on the pack animal. It takes practice to judge weight, and although many packers recommend carrying a scale into the mountains, not many actually do.

Panyards are great for the occasional packer who goes light, but if you do much packing and make longer trips, you'll soon experience their limitations: Unless they have very well designed flaps, panyards aren't very weather tight, and their flat tops tend to gather puddles and snow. Even good panyards will let in rain or spindrift when packed to their limit, as they invariably are at the start of a trip. This can be solved by covering them with a sheet of canvas held in place with a diamond hitch, but the convenience of panyards is considerably reduced by adding this extra step. Another drawback is fixed size. You can't take anything that won't fit in the panyard unless you tie it on top — diamond hitch again. The fixed size and shape also means that to use all the available space you have to tuck a lot of loose items into nooks and crannies, and loose items are often hard to find in the pack and easily lost. Panyards don't shrink as supplies are used up, either. If the mule packing in grain is supposed to pack out elk quarters, you're going to have to do something with his panyards.

None of these problems is all that serious. If it were, no one would use panyards. But together they make you wonder if there's not a better way. We think there is.

Figure 30a-b. In camp your manties can be put to all sorts of good uses.

a.

b.

Manties

The big advantage to mantying is versatility. The size and shape of loads can be adjusted to the items to be packed, and weights can be adjusted daily and to each horse's or mule's capacity without wasting space. Manties are easily loaded by one person and although they must balance, their shape permits considerable adjustment on the animal without unloading or rearranging gear. We'll explain this later when we show you how to load.

Equipment for mantying is virtually unbreakable and requires a smaller initial investment than panyards. You need only two sheets of canvas and two ropes. Properly folded, a manty holds a load together at least as well as a panyard and is more weatherproof. When you get to camp, tarps and ropes can be put to all sorts of additional uses. Manties can be used for cook tarps, wind screens, saddle covers and ground sheets. Smoke's wranglers usually sleep under manties. A good manty will keep you dry even on a very stormy night. You can even use them for refrigerators — wrap your butter and beer in a manty and sink it in the creek or hang everything in a

wet manty in a breezy location. Manty ropes can be used for corrals, clothes lines, guys and repairs. Because manties do double duty, they let you go further or stay longer without adding horses.

Manties are not without their drawbacks, not the least of which is that you have to know how to tie one up so you don't trickle gear along 20 miles of trail. Fear of just that, reinforced by the mystifying tangle of rope that holds a mantied load together, discourages many people from ever giving it a try. Actually mantying is easily learned and once mastered is easier and faster than loading panyards.

If you doubt this, consider that Smoke and one wrangler can manty and balance 20 loads, tie those loads on and be headed down the trail in less than an hour. We don't offer this as a goal you should aspire to, but we want you to know what's possible. You don't have to spend hours packing. There are better things to do in the mountains than pack and unpack, like ride, fish, hunt, eat or contemplate the sunset.

Another problem with mantying is that mantied gear is relatively inaccessible. To get something from a manty, you've got to unload the mule and take the manty apart. Good planning and saddle bags can reduce this problem to insignificance, but if you have a pack string of several horses or mules, you may find it convenient to pack one with panyards.

Most packers use seven by eight foot rectangles of 18 ounce canvas for their manties. Seven feet square is big enough, but canvas comes in eight foot widths. Canvas also comes in different weights. Anything between 12 ounce and 18 ounce is acceptable for manties. Lighter canvas tears and abrades too easily, while heavier canvas gets too stiff to fold when wet or frozen. We also recommend that you use untreated canvas. The treated duck is slightly more waterproof, but it will taint meat wrapped in it. Even if you're not a hunter, you may want the untreated material since a little air circulation is desirable when you have to pack wet gear. Don't try to use tarps made of synthetics. Plastics and nylon are too slippery to hold tight corners, and nylon in particular tends to snag on brush.

Manty ropes should be 30 to 35 feet long, back-spliced on one end and eye-spliced on the other (see Appendix II). A 100 foot roll will make three manty ropes. We use three-eighths inch or seven-sixteenths, soft-twist or spun nylon. Traditional wisdom holds that waxed manila is the only thing to use for sling, lash and manty ropes because it doesn't stretch much and holds knots very well. Nylon gets a bad rap because it does stretch and because the hard-twist nylon used in lariats doesn't hold knots at all. The advantages we see in nylon are that it is stronger, lasts longer, is easier on your hands and doesn't soak up

a.

b.

44

c.

Figure 31a-d. Coiling manty ropes so they're ready when you need them: a. coil the rope beginning with a loop in the loop end; b. wrap the loop completely around the coils; c. pass the loop through the coils; and d. pull tight.

d.

water, so it won't freeze under cold, snowy conditions. Stretch just isn't a problem at the tensions you'll be using; there's more give in the mantied load than in the rope. And spun nylon does hold knots well, particularly after it's begun to fray.

You can improve new manila manty ropes by training them before use. Drag new ropes for half a mile or so down a dirt road behind a pickup or a car. Stretch both manila and nylon by hand, wrapping them around two corral posts, and leave them there in the weather for a few days. If it doesn't rain, hose them down. This treatment puts a little fuzz on them and lessens their tendency to kink or stretch. Figure 31 shows our way of coiling manty ropes so they're quickly ready for use. When you're loading, tuck the loop end of a couple through your belt, and you'll have them when you need them.

Figure 32. Dropping a manty flat. The trick is to step back.

How To Manty

The first step in mantying up a load is to unfold two manties. You want them to be fairly flat, but don't run around straightening every wrinkle. With a little practice you can learn to shake out a folded manty and drop it so that it falls flat nearly every time. The trick is to step back as you drop it (Figure 32).

Now begin arranging gear along the diagonal of each manty. The items lying directly on the manty will be against the horse (unless you're going to use a barrel hitch) so try to start with something soft like a tent or a sleeping pad that can be folded to about the length and width of the finished load as padding. As you add to each pile there are three things you want to keep in mind. First, you want the two loads to be within five pounds of each other. Each item should be matched with an item of equal weight on the other manty. Second, you need an idea of the shape of the finished load. Although mantying allows considerable latitude in shaping the load, the height of the pack animal and the design

Figure 33. Arranging gear on a manty. Soft items go on the bottom. The heaviest items go down one third and out one third.

of the pack saddle impose practical limits. The ideal manty is about 36 inches long, 22 inches wide, and 16 inches thick, but it's easier to imagine your load taking the size and shape of a hay bale. You'll have no problems if the width is between 16 and 24 inches, the length 30 to 40 inches and the thickness, which isn't very critical, from five to 24 inches. Keep those limits in mind when buying equipment.

Finally, you have to think about how you're going to distribute the weight. The key item is the heaviest one in the load, that cannonball you suspect is in your mother-in-law's duffle bag. If you're a backpacker, you might imagine that you want that cannonball as high as you can get it, but you'd be wrong. Most packers will tell you to put it low, at the bottom of the load. That's a better choice than the top, but we think they're wrong, too. Smoke always says that the heavy item should be at "a third and a third." This means that the center of your cannonball should be one third of the way down from the top of the load and should be in the center third of the load coming out from the mule. In this position, the weight rides on the tree of the saddle and directly under the sling rope when you use a basket hitch.

Weight at either end exerts leverage which accentuates sway. By focusing the weight at "a third and a third," you minimize the load's sway, and you also insure that two loads of equal weight actually balance. This sounds like a contradiction since equal loads will always balance on a scale — but not on a mule or horse. If a mantied load with the weight on the bottom is loaded on a mule's left side and a load of equal weight but with the weight concentrated at the top is loaded on the right side, the saddle will sag to the left.

To help you visualize how loads are made up, Figure 34a-d takes you through the mantying process step by step.

a) Give the bottom corner a tug to get rid of wrinkles under the load. (Remember the load has a top and a bottom because of the way you arrange the weight.) Fold this corner up over the load.

b) Kneel on the bottom corner, and take the edge of the manty about 8 inches from the corner in your left hand. Pull it to the left and slightly up so that the manty folds smoothly along the horizontal edge.

Figure 34. Steps in fold and tying up a manty. (See text for explanation of each step.)

a.

b.

c.

d.

c) Still holding the manty with your left hand, grab the same edge with your right hand about 18 inches beyond your left hand and pull up and back toward your right shoulder to form a tight, square corner at the bottom of the load. This movement is awkward at first, but once you try it and see how it works, it's easy. Turn around and

repeat steps b anc c on the other bottom corner. Remember that left and right are now interchanged.

d) Finish by making a rainflap with the top corner of the manty. Since no weight rides on the top, you don't need a particularly tight corner here. Just tuck the excess in at the sides and fold the point down over the load, making a flap as wide as the load. Your manty will be neater if you fold the pointed tip of this rainflap under.

Try this a few times with a bale. You'll find it's easy to get a nice, tight manty. The rough canvas helps by holding itself in place between steps. There's nothing left now but tying it up. This isn't hard either, though some packers make it so. The process is illustrated in Figure 34e-h.

e) Holding the loop end of the manty rope throw the rest away from the bottom of the load. Form a loop big enough to go around the load's long axis. Tilt the load slightly on one long edge so that you can center this loop along the back and position the hondo or eye on the top edge. Then pull this loop tight. Tight means tight! You're going to pull **tight** after every step. Tightening will move the hondo about six inches down the load from the edge.

e.

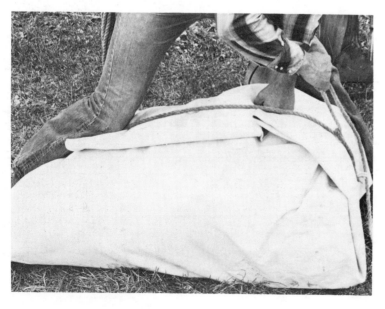

f.

g.

f) Smoke is about to throw a half hitch around the load six inches down from the top. Look carefully at how he has formed a loop in the picture. This looks very improbable when you go to do it. Have faith. If it doesn't work, you've probably formed the loop backwards. Go back to the picture and look carefully. Once you've thrown a few of these half hitches, the worst is over.

g) Smoke has turned around and has thrown a second and third half hitch in the center of the load and six inches from the bottom of the load respectively. Notice that these hitches center themselves when you pull. You may want to reverse every other half hitch so it tightens from alternate sides, but don't bother if this confuses you. If your load is short or solid, you may only need two half hitches, but three is better.

h) After tightening the last half hitch, Smoke wraps the loose end of the manty rope around the bottom, back and top of the load following the line of the loop he started with and arriving at last in the area of the eye splice and the first half hitch (the top front). All that's left to do now is tie off the loose end.

Figure 35a-d. Knot used to tie off a manty.

a.

b.

Figure 35 shows the knot we use to tie off a manty. Just about any knot that will stay tied will do the job, but ours has the advantage of being extrememly easy to untie: Just take the half hitch off the loop and pull the loose end. (The half hitch is only there to prevent the knot being accidentally untied if the loose end of the manty rope snags a tree.) Don't underestimate the importance of easy untying. When you have to make a camp in bad weather or in the dark, the last thing you want to do is struggle with knots. With the knot untied the manty practically unties itself. Since there are no pulled-through ropes, you simply throw off the half hitches, but drop each half hitch off the end it went on or you'll end up with knots in the rope.

Hitches For Loading

Before you can tie on the manties or panyards, your pack animal has to be

saddled. Presumably you already know how to saddle, but we're going to give you a saddling routine anyway. Again and again we see people who should know better saddling carelessly or incorrectly. We are also going to teach you three fundamental hitches for attaching loads: the basket hitch, the barrel hitch and the one-man diamond. There are literally dozens of good hitches in use among packers; among the best known are the box hitch, the squaw hitch, and innumerable diamond variations. Many of these have specialized applications, while the three we'll discuss are general enough that one of them will handle any load the average packer should ever need to carry. In fact, one, the basket hitch, is all some packers may ever need.

Begin saddling by placing the saddle and pad in front of the horse or mule where he can see it. Then brush him thoroughly. Besides cleaning him, this gives you an opportunity to check him out physically and mentally. If an animal got out of the

c.

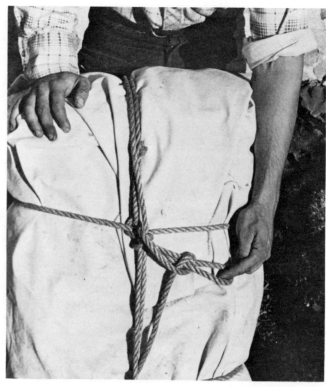

d.

Figure 36a-c. Quick release cinch knot.

wrong side of the bed, you have a chance to find out before entrusting him with the eggs. Check the saddle pad for crud: burrs, pine cones, sticks or grass seeds. Then put the pad on well ahead of the withers and slide it all the way back and off his rump. This aligns the hair on the back and if you have a fuzzy pile pad, it also aligns the nap. Now put the pad on ahead of the withers and slide it into position. On the average horse or mule, the leading edge of the pad should line up with the front of the foreleg. Two inches of pad should show ahead of the half-breed when the saddle is in position.

Now swing the saddle on. Nothing should be dangling (see chapter three for the recommended way to put up a pack saddle). The saddle tree is designed to fit in one particular place. The curve at the front of the tree fits the hollow just behind the withers. If you put the saddle ahead of this, it will pinch the shoulders and impede freedom of movement. If you put it too far

a.

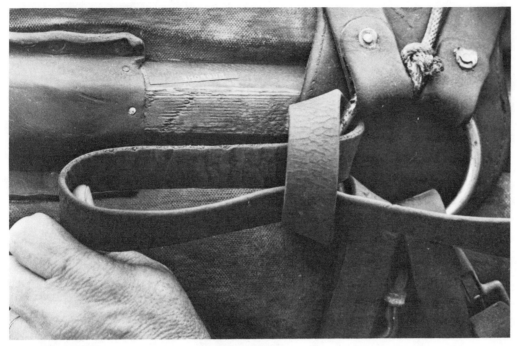

back, the tree will gouge the kidney area. Shake the saddle to seat it in the proper position.

Beginning with the breast collar, since that holds everything else up, start taking down the rigging. Let the breast collar hang. Check the off side to see that the latigo isn't twisted. Then come back around and cinch loosely, just tight enough to hold the saddle in place. You'll tighten it just before you load. We use a quick release cinch knot (Figure 36) so we can get the saddle off quickly in an emergency. It's just as secure as the standard knot. Now pull down and adjust the breeching (see the instructions in chapter three). Finally, hook up the breast collar.

Most mantied loads can be secured with the **basket hitch**, a very simple hitch and the one you'll use more than any other. Figure 37 shows the arrangement of sling ropes for the basket hitch. We keep our ropes threaded this way all the time.

Begin loading by placing the manties in front of the horse or mule and to either side so he can see what you're about to put on him. Give the rigging a last check, pull up

c.

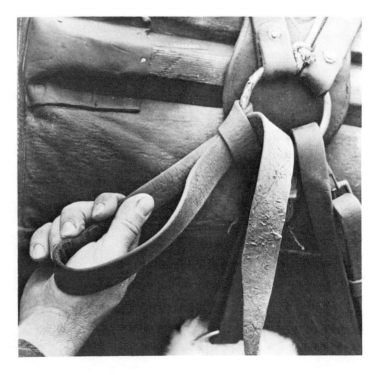

52

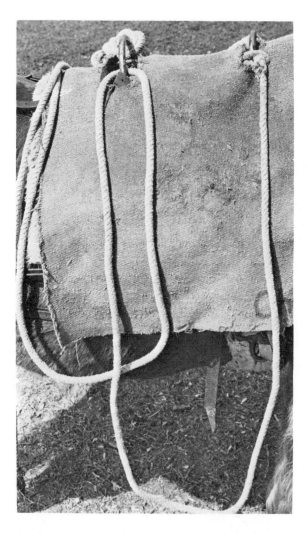

*Figure 37.
Sling rope
arrangement for
the basket hitch.*

the pad a little under the D-rings, and tighten the cinch. You want to pull it a little tighter than you would for a saddle horse. By the time you're a mile or two down the trail, the horse will have lost enough water in urine and sweat that the cinch will be loosening, and since you're not on him, you won't notice.

We have no handy rules to offer on how tight to cinch. Although such rules abound — a thumb here, three fingers there — we don't think any of them are worth much. Individual horses vary too much. The cinch has got to hold the saddle on without impairing breathing or causing sores. That means it has to be tight, even a little tighter than you would normally cinch a riding saddle, but just how tight this is depends on the individual horse or mule, the shape of his back and withers, his way of moving, and the tightness of his skin. Experience must be your guide. If you find puffiness or swelling along the girth line when you get to camp, the cinch was too tight.

*Figure 38.
Begin loading
by placing the loads
in front of the
pack horse or mule
so he can see what
you're about to put
on him. Notice
that two inches
of saddle pad
show ahead of
the half-breed.*

Figure 39a-c. Sequences showing how loads are attached with the basket hitch.

a. Place the load on the saddle in this position, centered front to back on the D-rings.

Pull down the sling rope. If you've put it up in the rear D-ring the way we showed you in chapter three, you don't have to untie anything. Just pull. Shape the section between the D-rings into a loop big enough to fit around the bottom of the manty when it's against the saddle. Experience will teach you how big this is. Drape the extra rope across the rump or neck. You don't want loose coils of rope on the ground where they can entangle you or your mule or be trampled into the mud. Struggling to get the loose end out from under one of your mule's big feet while you're holding up a 100-pound manty will do nothing for your disposition or your hernia.

Now you're ready to lift the load. Do this intelligently. One hundred pounds is a big load for anyone. Know what you can lift and lift it properly. Use your legs as much as possible, and try to keep your back fairly straight. If you injure your back or strain yourself in the back country, you're in trouble. Watch the horse or mule as you lift. You want to know what he's doing and where he is. Try to place the load in exactly the right position. That heaviest point — one third of the way down, remember? — rests against the saddle tree, and it should be centered between the two D-rings (Figure 39a).

Work the loop, which we hope you made large enough, up around the bottom of the load and position it so that it crosses that

b. Work the loop up and over the load, and position it as shown.

heaviest point. Tighten the loop in this position by pulling down on the loose end of the sling rope. It will be hanging down right in front of you but between the animal and the load where you can't see it. It helps the rope slide if you rock the load slightly from side to side between pulls. Pull hard. The load should be snugged up against the D-ring, though with a tall load you may have to leave it an inch or two away so the tops of the loads don't touch. All this will be easier if you support the load with your chest and upper arms as Smoke is doing in Figure 39c.

Once the loop is tight, you can bring the loose end up the tie off to the sling rope where it crosses the load. Don't tie to the manty rope! Use the knot in Figure 40a-d. This is another quick release knot like the one used to tie up a manty. There it was a convenience, here it is essential. If there's an accident, you want to be able to get loads off in a hurry.

Several years ago Smoke had an experience that illustrates the importance of this quick release feature. He was on his way out of the Bob Marshall Wilderness on the trail along the North Fork of the Blackfoot. A heavy storm in the morning had delayed his departure, and by the time his string of ten mules reached the narrow canyon near the trailhead, dusk was fading rapidly. A mule near the end of the string slipped and slid down the bank into the

c. Pull the loop tight and bring the rope up under the load and tie-off.

55

a.

b.

c.

Figure 40a-d. *Quick release knot used to tie-off the basket hitch. (The smaller diameter rope is the manty rope. Don't tie to it!)*

river, pulling two other mules with her. The North Fork is a fast mountain river, and the mules fell into a deep pool. Two got their legs tangled in ropes as they fell and the other was pinned beneath them under water. The loads of all three were taking water and growing heavier by the second.

Smoke was able to pull the loads off the top two mules so they could scramble free. Then he held the head of the third above water while one of his wranglers untied the loads. Smoke believes that his use of quick release knots saved at least one mule and possibly all three. His comment, "You couldn't cut rope fast enough," begs the question of whether you want to be wielding a knife at all in the midst of 3600 pounds of struggling mules.

When both loads are on, rock them from side to side a few times; then see if the D-rings center along the animal's back. If the saddle lists to one side or the other, and

d.

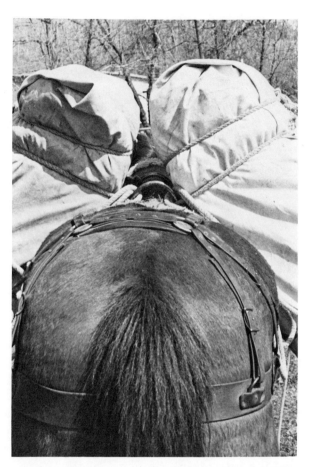

Figure 41. When the loads are balanced, the D-rings will center on the pack animal's back.

Figure 42a-b. Store extra sling rope in loops on the front and rear D-rings.

a.

you know the loads are balanced to within five or six pounds, you can adjust the balance by lowering the load on the light side or raising the load on the heavy side a little. Put up the extra rope in loops on the rear D-rings (Figure 42). This gets the extra rope out of the way and also lets you pull as much slack as you need for on-the-trail adjustments without untying all of it. You're done.

Many packers tie their basket-hitched loads down to the latigo or an extra ring on the end of the girth. This negates several of the advantages of the basket hitch, and we don't think that you should do it except under certain special circumstances. You may also see packers who have tied their loads together at the top. This is a bad idea all the time.

b.

Tied the way we've shown it, the basket hitch is free to swing forward and back. If an inexperienced pack animal comes too close to a tree, the load can swing back out of the way without upsetting anything. On hills, the loads swing forward or back aiding the mule's or horse's balance. Because manties are straight and ribs are curved, when you tie the bottom of a load down, you're putting extra pressure on the animal's ribs. If you've mantied rigid objects, you can

actually impair his breathing. Even if that doesn't happen, you're increasing the risk of sore ribs and possibly girth sores as well, since the tie pulls the girth away from the animal's side and makes it tighter across the brisket.

The only time you want to tie down a basket hitch is when you're traveling in country where your stock is forced to jump and lunge, for example in deep, drifted snow, muskeg or downed timber. Even then, don't tie too tightly, just tight enough that the loads don't flop.

Tying basket-hitched loads together at the top defeats all your efforts to get the weight in the right place. Pulling them in raises the center of gravity, increasing the tendency of the loads to sway, and prevents them from moving independently.

Use the basket hitch to pack front quarters of elk and halves of deer. Front quarters of elk should be loaded with the hide against the saddle and the leg pointing down and back. The left quarter must go on the mule's right side and vice versa. In this position the fleshy side is against the saddle and the ribs curve outward.

To cut a deer into halves of equal weight, remove the head and divide the deer between the second and third ribs, counting forward from the abdomen. (This is also the best place to divide an elk so that all four

58

*Figure 43.
Basket hitched
front quarters
of elk.*

quarters are approximately the same weight.) The front half, like the front quarter of an elk, is loaded with the legs to the rear, though in this case the side makes no difference. The back half of a deer is basket-hitched with the back against the saddle and the hocks down. The sling rope comes up between the hocks, which should be tied together either in the process of mantying or with a scrap of rope.

In cold weather it is not necessary to manty game, though a manty will help keep the meat clean. When flies are active, mantying is essential to prevent fly-blown meat. Most packers have special manties just for meat so their duffle manties don't become blood encrusted. A meat manty can

be smaller than a regular manty — four by five feet is a good size — and need not be canvas. Heavy cotton cloth will work well and is much cheaper. Don't wrap meat in plastic or garbage bags unless both the weather and the meat are cold. Even on a cool day, if the sun is shining, plastic will absorb heat and speed spoilage.

The **barrel hitch** is another very simple hitch, but it takes a little more time to adjust and tie than the basket hitch. The principle use of this hitch is in packing pointed or odd shaped objects that lack a blunt surface adequate to hold the bottom rope of a basket hitch. Hindquarters of elk (Figure 44) are a good example, as are barrels and fence posts.

*Figure 44.
Barrel hitched
hind-quarters
of elk.*

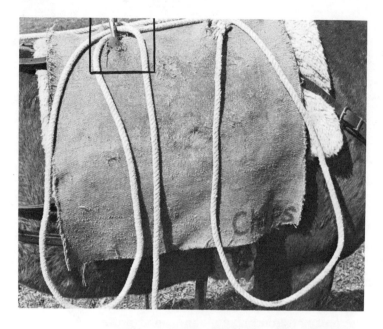

Figure 45. (with inset)
Sling rope arrangement
for the barrel hitch.

The correct sling rope arrangement for the barrel hitch is pictured in Figure 45. Before you load this hitch, be sure that when the loose end of the rope comes back through the rear D-ring after forming the final loop, it runs on top of the section of rope coming from the front D-ring. If it doesn't, you may have trouble adjusting the rear loop.

Loading this hitch is simply a matter of suspending the mantied load in the two loops and adjusting it to the proper position. The heavy end of the load goes in the front loop, and the rainflap of the manty goes in, against the half-breed. The front end of the load should be one to two inches higher than the back, and the back should not extend beyond the rear edge of the half-breed or it will rub the pack animal's hip. Here again, you want the weight carried on the tree of the saddle. Instead of tightening the sling loops until the load is against the D-rings, leave them loose enough so that the top of the load hangs level with the top of the saddle or the base of the D-rings.

Unlike the basket hitch, the barrel hitch can be tied down. Tying down a barrel hitch doesn't affect the balance of the load, and because the sling loops aren't tight around it, tying a load increases its security. Once the load is positioned correctly, bring the loose end of the sling rope up from beneath the load and thread it under the section of sling rope where it runs between the two D-rings. Notice that this is the first time we've told you to use a pulled-through rope. That's a disadvantage to this hitch. Now go to the lash ring on the girth if there is one; if there isn't, you can thread the rope through the outer wrap of latigo. If you're short or your sling rope is, you may want to tie off here with a quick-release knot. Otherwise, go back up over the load and tie off on top between the D-rings. This can be a long reach, but it puts your knot where it's not likely to be snagged by a stick or a bush. Loop any extra rope through the rear D-ring the way we showed you before, and you're done. Figure 46 shows a correctly loaded barrel hitch.

Don't worry about tying to the latigo instead of a lash ring. If you made a couple of turns with the latigo before you tied your

cinch knot and the cinch is tight, this piece of latigo can break and your saddle will stay tight for quite a while. You should notice the load slipping long before the saddle starts to slip.

Barrel-hitched hind quarters of elk, like front quarters, should be loaded with the left quarter on the mule's right side and the right quarter on the mule's left side. The legs, which should be cut off just below the hock, point to the rear and slightly up.

Barrel hitched hindquarters of elk provide an ideal platform for packing elk antlers. Packing antlers has been one of the most enduring problems to plague packers. The traditional solution has been to straddle the horse or mule, carrying front quarters, with the rack, points to the rear. This works for big racks, but not all racks will fit this way. Whats more, the tines can gouge a big hole in your animal should she fall over.

Figure 46. A barrel-hitched load. Smoke will tie-off to the sling rope between the D-rings.

a.

*Figure 47a-b.
Top-packed
elk antlers,
using barrel
hitched loads
as a platform.*

Our solution appears in Figure 47. With the points up and back, not only will they not stab your pack animal, but they should travel without snagging on brush or overhanging branches. This position mimics the way a bull elk carries his antlers through the woods.

To pack antlers this way, use the extra sling rope on one side, pull a bight through the front D-ring and loop it over both brow tines. Pull tight, and tie it off with several half hitches around both the hock-joint of the hindquarter and the last fork of the antler. Tie the other hock to the other side of the rack with the other sling rope. Not only does this make a very stable load, but the hocks, tied tightly to the antlers, are pulled away from the mule's hips so they can't rub a sore. In fact, if you aren't packing antlers, you should adjust each quarter carefully so that it doesn't rub against the pack animal's hip or neck.

b.

*The stick, shown
in b, is not always
needed, but it
provides a better
platform and with
smaller racks,
helps hold hock
joints away from
the pack animal's
hips.*

Figure 48a-c. Packing a riding saddle. Use one sling rope (half on each side). Pull the mid-point of the rope through the saddle fork and attach the horn as shown in a.

a.

It is possible to pack a riding saddle using either the barrel hitch or the basket hitch. Figure 48 shows the sling rope arrangement for each. When using either, you should take care that the load does not damage the saddle. A basket-hitched load on a riding saddle should be positioned behind the swells of the saddle. A barrel-hitched load rides below the swells. Otherwise, a solid load will wear away the leather. We don't recommend that you make a practice of packing your riding saddle, simply because of this potential for damage.

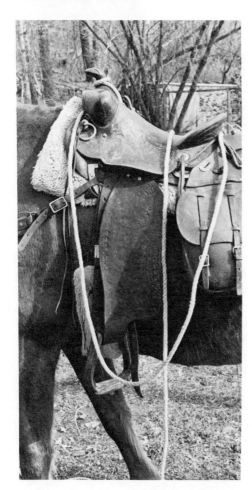

b. Basket hitch.

c. Barrel hitch.

Figure 49. A lash cinch.

Still, knowing how to pack a riding saddle can be useful in a pinch and invaluable for hunters. Packing elk requires two pack animals, so being able to pack your saddle horse can sometimes save an extra round trip between game and camp. Elk quarters go on a riding saddle just as they do on a pack saddle. However, when a deer is to be packed on a riding saddle, it is easiest not to divide it at all. Instead, cut a slit in the skin of the belly at the tip of the third rib, and with the deer draped over the saddle, buttonhole this slit over the saddle horn. Clove-hitch a length of rope to the horn so that half hangs down each side of the horse. Throw a half-hitch around the deer on each side and tie to the outer wrap of the latigo. In this position, the deer should balance well and should stay in the middle of your horse's back as long as the half-hitches are tight.

The **diamond hitch** is a specialized hitch used for top packing. Top packing is standard practice with sawbuck pack saddles. In the old west, a prospector's donkey without a diamond hitch across his load would have looked naked. Now, because the Decker pack saddle with mantied loads allows a horse or mule to be easily loaded to capacity, the diamond hitch has become an anachronism, at least in the Northwest. Most Montana outfitters will add a mule rather than top pack. In Wyoming, Colorado and points south, where more packers use sawbucks and panyards, top packing with the diamond hitch is still standard procedure. You may want to learn it even if you've decided to pack with manties. The diamond is so much a part of western lore that being able to throw it amounts to an initiation rite into the fraternity of packers. Someday you may want to top pack, if only to get more hay to your hunting camp than you could otherwise.

We strongly recommend that you top pack only light loads, in no case greater than three fourths the weight of one side load. Hay bales are a permissible exception if they are light, say 50 pounds. Usually you'll want to top pack some bulky item like a stove, or a tent that didn't match up when you were mantying or couldn't be made to fit in your panyards. Too much weight on top gets the center of gravity too high, and all that weight bearing straight down on the D-rings or cross bucks can be hard on your saddle.

Think of the diamond as a cargo net that holds the entire load together and ties directly to the animal, not the saddle, via a lash cinch. A lash cinch is a leather or canvas girth, longer and wider than a saddle girth with a ring at one end and a hook at the other. You'll also need a lash rope 40 to 45 feet long and three-eighths to one-half inch in diameter. This can be eye-spliced directly to the ring of the lash cinch or looped on with the eye-splice so you can remove the rope and use it later in camp. You should also have something to cover your loads before you throw the diamond. A square of canvas between four and six feet square is the size you'll need, but a folded manty or canvas tent works just as well. This cover waterproofs the load, and it also helps keep your lash rope separate from the sling ropes and the manty ropes underneath. Obviously the diamond requires a considerable amount of extra gear.

The diamond will seem complicated the first few times you tie it. Although we refer to "the diamond," there are several specialized variations of the diamond idea and many routines for tying it. The one we've chosen to teach you — primarily because it is as simple as any — is the one-man diamond.

The one-man diamond tying sequence is illustrated in Figure 50a-i.

a) Smoke has top packed some duffle over two mantied and barrel-hitched bales and is throwing the pack cover over the load.

a.

Figure 50a-i.
The diamond hitch.

b.

Notice that the lash rope begins on the horse's right side and crosses the top of the load.

b) Starting with the loose end of the lash rope hanging down along the horse's right shoulder, lay the rope over the top load and down the middle of the horse's back. Stand on the left side of the horse and form a four to six foot loop through the ring of the lash cinch.

c) Holding the end of the loop, throw the lash cinch across the load, catch the end as it comes under the horse and hook it onto the loop. It can be a big reach to the lash cinch under the horse. If you can't reach it safely, go around the horse and start it swinging. Even though this is a one-man diamond, a partner helps.

d) Go to the right side of the horse and tighten and adjust the position of the lash cinch. It should come up the same distance on each side of the horse. At this point the cinch only needs to be snug. It will get tighter as the diamond is tied. You don't want it to loosen as you work though, so it's a good idea to tie it off with a half hitch, as shown, the first few times you try the diamond.

c.

d.

e.

e) Two strands of the lash rope come across the top of the load with the single strand of the loose end crossing at a right angle under them. Twist the two parallel strands over each other three or four times, then pull a loop of the single strand up between them.

f) Starting at the cinch ring on the right side, place the lash rope along the bottom and back side of the load and tighten it adding the slack to the loop you formed (in e) on top.

f.

g.

g) Now go the left side of the horse. Place the loop down around the bottom of the load on this side. Make the loop as big as you need to do this. Pull on it where it comes from between the twisted ropes and the diamond will begin to open up. Work it tight all the way around the load on this side.

h) Go to the right side again and pull on the loose end which should still be hanging by the horse's right foreleg. This opens up the diamond completely. Position the rope under the lower front corner of the load, and tie off to the ring of the lash cinch. You may have to go once more around the horse tightening the hitch at each corner of the load as you go. Pull hard.

i) The finished product.

You now have the basic techniques to pack anything you're likely to want to take into the mountains. If you respect your pack animal's limitations and learn to apply the basic principles of weight distribution and balance, you're on your way to being able to pack anything that can be packed. Smoke's adventure with the piano is a good example of what's possible.

Smoke was once asked to pack a piano to a backcountry cabin nine miles from the

h.

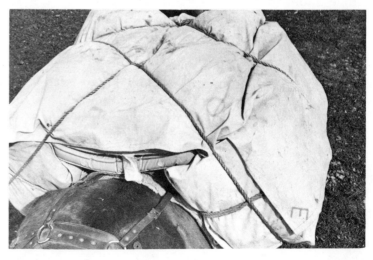

i.

nearest road. He agreed to try even though the problems were considerable. The trail wasn't particularly steep, but it did cross a mountain ridge, and though the piano was a small upright model, it weighed nearly 400 pounds.

To support the piano, Smoke built a four-foot square plywood platform, mounted on two-by-sixes bolted across the D-rings of a Decker. To lift the piano onto the saddle, he cut three lodgepole pines and made a tripod for a block and tackle that allowed him to lift the piano eight feet off the ground. He chose an 1800-pound, half-Lippizaner work mare and recruited two assistants to help with the tripod.

At the trailhead they laid the piano on its side and padded the strings so they wouldn't sound as the horse walked. Then they wrapped the piano in furniture pads and trussed it in lash ropes that all tied into a heavy cinch ring. The ring gave a single point that could be hooked onto the block and tackle. When the piano was first lowered onto the mare's back, the platform tipped severely to one side or the other. To stabilize it, Smoke ran a lash cinch under the mare and tied it to the edges of the platform. The piano was held in place with rubber lashings cut from an inner tube.

Once they saw that the piano would ride safely, Smoke led the mare while the other two rode ahead with a pack mule dragging the tripod. Every half mile or so, depending on the terrain, they would stop and set up the tripod. The mare who quickly learned what it was for, would see it, perk up her ears and hustle to get underneath. The piano would be raised, the mare would get a rest and sometimes a drink. Then she was loaded and the routine was repeated. They covered the nine miles in a long day and the piano arrived at the cabin with only a few rope burns to show for its ordeal. It's still there.

Figure 51. *A camp is less a place than a collection of gear that allows you to be comfortable in the hills.*

Harley Hettick

chapter five
Camp Equipment

As employed by packers, the term "camp" refers less to a place than to the items of food, clothing, shelter and tools brought to that place and used there. The basic needs are the same as those provided by your home, but in deciding to go camping, you're choosing to live for a while with fewer conveniences and less amenity than usual. Yet camping does not mean you have to endure a spare existence at the edge of survival. The satisfaction in camping comes from getting along comfortably with less. How well you succeed depends on your equipment, skill and experience. To the extent that you rely on skill, camping is a game; but it's a game in which you choose in advance the level at which you wish to play.

With a pack string, you can carry a more comfortable camp than you can with a backpack. How much you exploit this advantage depends on your need for comfort, your skill, the size of your string and your feelings about how the game should be played. The equipment and supplies you take into the hills should reflect your sense of what is appropiate and satisfying in the backcountry.

We would like to leave the size and content of your camp entirely to your taste and discretion. With American society becoming more homogenized, our wild country should remain a refuge for individualism. Unfortunately, one effect of more and more people in the backcountry is

that extremes of taste can be destructive of wilderness. So can the regulations that inevitably follow abuses. Use good sense and moderation in the hills, if only to preserve your freedom.

The right amount of good equipment does more than permit you to live comfortably; it let's you be light on the land. You can always take more by adding horses to your string, but the tradeoff is that more horses are more trouble and do more damage. You will enjoy the greatest mobility and do the least damage if you limit yourself to a light camp. Light means light by packhorse standards; the extreme weight economies of backpacking are unnecessary. You are not confined to dried foods and synthetic materials, much less a filed-down tooth brush and one towel per party. A pack horse or mule, depending on his size, can carry 150 to 200 pounds, making one pack horse per rider a generous maximum. Pack animals should be loaded to capacity. Underloading stock means you'll have to take more of them. If for any reason a horse or mule can't carry a full load, the animal shouldn't be taken into the hills.

If it is poor style and destructive to take too much, it is equally so to take too little. On a pack trip there's no excuse for not taking adequate clothing, shelter and food. We believe it is wrong to employ survival techniques in order to travel light. Too many people are using the back-country for

a. A-frame

Figure 52a-d. Four basic types of tent.

any packer to depend on the land for needs that could easily be supplied by his camp. It may seem romantic to go into the mountains with only a blanket, a few matches and a fish hook, but except in the most remote areas, you'll use more than your fair share of the available firewood, fish and small game. A few hungry campers can wipe out a covy of mountain grouse with nothing more lethal than rocks and walking sticks.

Except for this caution about extremes, we have no intention of dictating what you should take. In this chapter we want to give you a sense of the possibilities for a camp, while sharing some of our ideas about what equipment works well and why. If you've done any camping at all, whether backpacking or car camping, you probably have all the equipment you need to begin camping with stock. We suggest you start with what you already have. Buy new equipment only when you can't make do. As you gain experience and develop preferences, you can add to or make substitutions in your outfit.

Shelter

Tents are a barrier between you and your surroundings, but prolonged bad weather, bugs and long winter nights make them a necessary evil. If you're going to do much camping in the mountains, you'll need one. You don't always have to use it, and if you're like us, you'll often leave it packed. A little dew or frost on your sleeping bag is a small price for a night of stars wheeling overhead. But tempt fate by going into the

b. Teepee or pyramid

c. Dome

The Trailhead

d. Wall tent

mountains without a tent, and you can bet the ranch it will rain for three days or giant mosquitoes will emerge at dusk and fly away with you.

Tents come in a bewildering array of shapes, sizes, designs, weights and materials. Figure 52a-d shows four different types: the A-frame, the pyramid or teepee, the dome, and the traditional wall tent. Virtually all the tents available are variations on or hybrids of these basic themes. Each design has its advantages; none is perfect. But with so many to choose from, you should, with a little effort, be able to choose a tent that suits your needs and — less certainly — your bankroll.

Tents aren't cheap. Good ones cost between $125 and $400. Cheaper models are rarely bargains. Because materials, design and workmanship tend to be inferior, inexpensive tents sag in rain and snow and flap badly in the wind. Even if an inexpensive tent is strong enough to withstand such strains, you probably aren't. After a few hours in a luffing, snapping tent, you'll be flapping in the breeze yourself.

Besides cost, there are a number of general features to consider in choosing any tent:

Tents used by packers span a wide range in weight — from five to ten pounds for lightweight backpacking tents to 80 or 100 pounds for the heaviest canvas wall tents. Even confining yourself to the lower half of this range, you can satisfy any reasonable requirement for space and comfort. In Smoke's outfit, which provides considerable comfort for his guests, tentage makes up 20 percent of the total load. There's no reason for you to exceed this, and you can probably do better. If you have a 1000 pound pack horse or mule, the weight of your tents and flies should not exceed 40 pounds.

Next, get a tent that is big enough to be comfortable. Just because a tent is marketed as a "two-man" model doesn't mean it is. A two-person tent should have ample room for two and all their gear. Don't take the manufacturer's word for this. Before you buy, put the tent up, get in and crawl around until you're satisfied it's large enough. You should be able to dress without elbowing your tentmate and sit without touching the tent. Better still get a tent that let's you stand. Your lumbago will love you for it, and it will be easier to fend off claustrophobia when a prolonged storm keeps you inside.

You have a choice of materials between nylon and cotton. The best nylon tents are made of "ripstop," an aptly named weave with enormous resistance to tearing. It is easy to recognize "ripstop" by its faint checkered pattern. Heavier threads spaced one quarter inch apart give "ripstop" its strength without adding much weight. Besides being strong and light, nylon is slippery and sheds snow well. It can be packed wet for several days without beginning to rot or mildew. But because of its thinness and hard finish, nylon is easily abraded. A nylon tent should be packed in a rugged stuff sack to prevent sling ropes and hard objects in the load from wearing holes in it. The stuff sacks provided with nylon tents are often too light.

Cheaper nylon tents are often made entirely of coated waterproof material. With one expensive exception, which we'll discuss in a moment, you shouldn't waste your money on a coated tent. Only the floor and lower walls of a nylon tent should be waterproof. Coated tents will keep you dry in a brief shower, but after an all-night rain, you'll be as wet as if you'd slept outside. Waterproof nylon traps body moisture from breath and sweat in the tent. This moisture condenses on the roof and walls and rains back down on your sleeping bag. The solution is to use a coated rainfly in combination with an uncoated tent. Water vapor passes through the tent and condenses on the fly where it runs off harmlessly. Good quality nylon tents come with rain flies.

The one exception is tents made with Gore-Tex®. Gore-Tex® is a porous teflon-like film which is laminated to nylon, proofing it against rain but not against water vapor. The microscopic pores are far smaller than droplets of liquid water, but allow water vapor given off by your body to pass through easily. The teepee tents Smoke uses on his summer trips are Gore-Tex®, and they work very well. Gore-Tex® is expensive though. It adds 25 to 30 percent to the price of a comparable tent made of uncoated ripstop.

Cotton tents can be made of canvas, but the best are poplin or drill. These weaves are durable, easy to handle and lighter than canvas. All have a tendency to be self-waterproofing. As the fabric gets wet, the cotton threads swell, sealing the holes in the weave. Cotton tents should be treated with a good waterproofing compound, and seams should be sealed. Waterproofing doesn't last indefinitely, and touching the tent reduces its effectiveness. In the long run, you'll be happier with your cotton tent if you use a waterproof fly pitched on a separate ridgepole, four to six inches above the tent. This space allows good air

circulation. Wet cotton tents should be dried as soon as possible or they begin to mildew and rot.

Use a light-colored fly with your cotton tent. Though nylon tents of any color are transluscent, cotton materials are less so. We have seen packers using black plastic for a rainfly. It's cheap and waterproof but very dark. Unless you find the idea of living in a cave attractive, we suggest that you buy tents and flies in light colors. They will be cooler in summer too.

All tents, both nylon and cotton, should be treated with a fire retardant. Untreated nylon tents are illegal in many states; they will ignite into a conflagration within seconds. Cotton isn't as inflammable as nylon, but it will burn. Not all cotton tents are treated. Some manufacturers offer retardant treatment as an option which adds about 25 percent to the weight of a tent and 10 percent to its cost.

The difference between a good tent and a poor one lies in design and construction. Good tents, when pitched, are tight. Sagging and wrinkles indicate bad design or poor workmanship. Stress points (seams, guy attachments, and pole fittings) should be reinforced and well stitched. Upright poles that bear directly on the tent are bad. When the tent is loaded by snow, wind or even rain, such poles may spear through the fabric.

Finally, a good tent is easy to set up. Sooner or later you'll have to put it up in the dark or in a high wind. Then millions of pegs and hard-to-assemble poles can drive you to despair.

The **A-frame** tent is a descendant of the venerable pup tent. It is a proven design that remains popular despite innovative competition. A-frame tents are light, moderately easy to erect, and stable in wind. These characteristics make them popular among backpackers and mountaineers, so most models are fairly small. The sloping roof results in wasted space and tends to sag rather than shedding snow. Traditional A-frames require guy ropes and lots of pegs, making them hard to pitch securely on sand and snow. Freestanding variations employing exterior frames minimize these problems. Most larger A-frame tents have exterior frames and some of these are large enough to stand up in.

Pyramid or **teepee style** tents have lost partisans to the recently developed domes. Marketing may have something to do with this since the pyramid style is simple, easy to pitch, and efficient for larger groups. Pictured is the Gortex® teepee tent Smoke manufactures and uses for his summer trips. It requires only four pegs, a single pole and no guy lines. It allows you to stand, a feature not shared by any dome that we know of.

The **dome** is both the newest and possibly the oldest type of tent. The modern incarnation is inspired by the space efficiency and strength of the geodesic dome, but the nomadic tribes of Central Asia have used the yurt, a similar structure, for thousands of years. Domes are at least as strong and stable as A-frames. They are also self-supporting and offer much usable space for their weight. They are probably the most comfortable of the low-ceilinged tents, but because they are designed for the backpacking and mountaineering markets, none allow you to stand. The larger domes have ceilings 50 to 54 inches high. Domes can also be hard to put up. In some, up to 36 pole sections have to be assembled. Most makers simplify this situation by linking sections with shock cord or sewing them into the tent. We suggest that before you buy a dome, you try setting it up. Some pitch much more easily than others. Like other self-supporting tents, a dome can be picked up and moved to a more comfortable site after it has been set up.

The **wall** tent has been the packer's traditional choice for hunting camps and winter use. A wall tent can be modified to permit use of a small heating and cooking stove, and the size and shape of a wall tent lets you walk around — welcome features on long, cold winter nights. By mid-November in the Northern Rockies, there are 14 and a half hours between sunset and sunrise. That's a long time to stay huddled in your sleeping bag.

Besides being roomy and warm, wall tents are rugged, strong and versatile. Pitched properly with ridgepoles, they can withstand heavy wind and snow loads.

*Figure 53.
One of Smoke's
Gore-tex®
teepee tents.*

Several tents can be linked to form comfortable permanent camps for large parties. The diagram in Figure 55 shows the arrangement Smoke uses for his hunting camps (see Figure 52d for a photograph). This set-up gives a central kitchen and gathering area separate from the sleeping areas. The cook can start an early breakfast and warm the tents without waking anyone else up.

Wall tents weigh anywhere from 12 pounds for nylon models to 80 pounds for very large canvas tents. Smoke's wall tents with a 14x16 floor area are made of drill and weigh 35 to 40 pounds.

Many wall tents come without floors. This isn't necessarily bad. Manties can be laid out to make a floor — don't let them protrude under the wall of the tent where they can collect water — and a piece of indoor-outdoor carpet rolled out down the center of the tent gives a warm surface to walk around on. Such a removable floor can be taken outside and shaken clean. It also can be arranged so the stove rests on bare ground.

To use a stove safely, you'll have to modify your wall tent to let the stovepipe pass through the roof. If you just cut a hole and stick the pipe through, you're going to burn down your tent, possibly with you in it. Where the pipe comes through, you must replace the fabric with a firestop.

Some tents come equipped with fireproof chimney holes, but holes are easily added to tents that don't have them. Figure 54 shows how firestops are fitted in Smoke's wall tents. A rectangular hole, approximately 18 inches by 24 inches is cut in the roof with

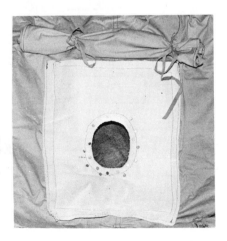

*Figure 54.
Firestop
for stove pipe
in one of
Smoke's wall tents.*

the long dimension running up and down. The hole is filled with a double layer of rubberized asbestos cloth having a round hole cut to fit a five or six inch stovepipe tightly. The rectangular cut out piece of Camper Cloth® is then sewn above the firestop with ties to keep it out of the way. When the tent is used without a stove, this flap is rolled down to cover the opening.

Some people simply sandwich the tent roof between the two layers of fireproof material. We don't recommend this method of installation because we have seen one instance where the tent roof, left between the fireproof layers, began to smolder and burned to the edge of the firestop where, fortunately, it went out.

Metal firestops are also available, and if you are uncomfortable with having asbestos, even sealed in rubber, above your cook stove, this is your best alternative. A metal firestop is quickly and easily installed in an open seam. If it isn't positioned properly, however, it can get in the way when the tent is folded, and may wear holes in the tent.

The Forest Service has investigated fire resistant materials for firefighters and has found some, like high-temperature-resistant silicone rubber moulded over fiberglass cloth, that would make excellent firestops. But getting these materials in small quantities can be extremely difficult.

There are two other dangers associated with using a wood stove in a tent that require precautions. Every year someone dies in a tightly-battened tent with a smoldering stove. If your wall tent doesn't have vents under the eaves, you should cut them there. These provide necessary ventilation with very little heat loss. Should

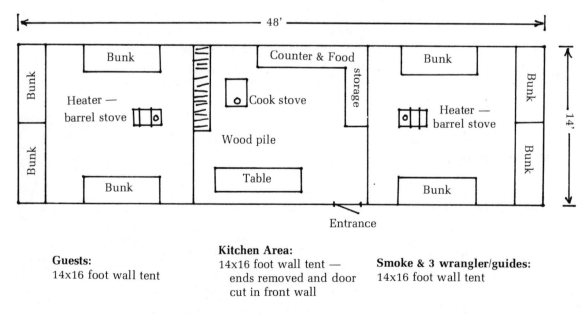

Guests:
14x16 foot wall tent

Kitchen Area:
14x16 foot wall tent —
   ends removed and door
   cut in front wall

Smoke & 3 wrangler/guides:
14x16 foot wall tent

Figure 55. Diagram of Smoke's hunting camp.

a.

your stove pipe be blocked or leak during the night, the smoke can escape. In a smaller tent, you may also want to sew a square of asbestos cloth to the tent behind the stove. In any case, a stove should be at least 36 inches from the wall.

Some old-time packers carry an extra tent to protect tack and assorted gear, but an extra waterproof tarp, either canvas or synthetic, is all you need. We stack saddles on a manty, cover them with a tarp and tuck

Figure 56a-b.
Stacking and
covering saddles
for protection
from weather and
rodents.

b.

*Figure 57.
Smoke in
his kitchen.*
Harley Hettick

it in under the manty. This arrangement is also an effective rodent deterrent. Porcupines, pack rats, marmots and flying squirrels all gnaw leather. Give a porcupine an hour and he can destroy your $500 saddle.

Because we often have to cook outdoors in bad weather, we carry a kitchen fly (see Figure 51). Even in good weather, a fly produces welcome shade against the late afternoon sun. We like a kitchen tarp big enough to drop one side against the wind. Ten by 12 feet will shelter four to six people. The material is up to you. Smoke's kitchen tarp is drill; mine is coated nylon. Plastic is cheaper than either and works well, but is less durable and may crack in cold weather.

Kitchens

Like his camp, the packer's kitchen isn't a place as much as a collection of equipment used to turn out meals. The term usually encompasses food as well, but here we're going to confine ourselves to kitchen equipment. Professional outfitters take great pride in their kitchens — understandably, since meal-time satisfaction can bring back guests year after year.

If you're just starting out as a packer, your kitchen can be as simple as a few old pots, a frying pan and some utensils scavenged from home. After you've packed for a while, particularly if you travel with groups of four or more, you'll inevitably find yourself building a more complex kitchen — unless you hate to cook and would rather get along on the simplest of menus. There's not much we can tell you if that's the case. The rest of us like to eat, and riding all day builds up ravenous appetites. Your horse isn't doing all the work.

A minimum kitchen for one or two people includes two pots — four and six quart are good sizes — a frying pan or griddle, and a coffee pot. For bigger groups it's nice to add two more pots, maybe in two and eight quart sizes. The Boy Scouts and many sporting good stores sell large-group cook kits with approximately this aray of pots and pans. These also include plates and cups for six or eight people.

Most camp cook kits are made of aluminum. Aluminum undeniably has its virtues: it's light and the price is right. But aluminum also dents easily, and lacking a hard, smooth surface, is hard to clean.

Smoke, whose kitchen is in constant use from mid-June to late November, prefers stainless steel cookware. The added ruggedness — horses have stepped on some of his pots without inflicting noticeable damage — and ease of clean-up more than compensate for the extra cost and weight. The trade-offs between aluminum and stainless steel are clearcut. You can make your own choice.

In addition to your cooking pots, a basin or two can be useful for dishwashing, shaving; even cooking in a pinch. Plastic dishwashing basins are the lightest, but they require diverting a pot from cooking for heating water. Metal basins are more versatile, since you can put them directly on the fire or stove. Here we feel stainless has a definite advantage, though enamelware is a good second choice. A basin you shave over

in the morning and boil potatoes in at night must rinse easily. It takes a lot of scrubbing and rinsing to get the last little bit of shaving soap and beard off the porous surface of aluminum. A good, warm-water rinse will get you to the same point with stainless.

You'll also need plates and silverware. We like hard plastic plates better than metal. They may be slightly harder to get grease-free, but cutting meat on plastic isn't like running fingernails across a blackboard, and the plastic is easier on your hunting knife. Plastic also keeps your food hotter longer. Metal plates are often too hot to hold and they quickly dissipate the warmth of your meal to cold air. You can use paper plates if you wish, but we don't think its good style to import the throwaway habit into the mountains.

The case for plastic cups is less clearcut.

Figure 58.
A pair of
stainless steel
wash basins.

Some softer plastics give drinks a plastic or soapy taste. Hard plastic cups less often have this defect. Metal cups, like metal plates, lose heat rapidly and burn your lips when filled with hot coffee. The stainless steel Sierra Club cup reduces this hazard by. including a steel bale in the rim which protrudes to form the handle. For some reason the rim stays tolerably cool, but don't let your lips touch any other part of the cup.

We suggest you carry an extra set of silverware. This may not be necessary in a party of one or two, but the incidence of lost knives, forks and spoons increases geometrically with the size of your group.

A good assortment of kitchen tools includes: a long-handled spatula, two to four stirring and serving spoons, a long-handled fork, one or two sharp slicing knives, a potato peeler, a pliers-type can opener, and a cork screw. You also want a pot grabber, a pair of pot holders or white work gloves (gloves are better if you're cooking over an open fire), two to four cloth dish towels (handy even if you carry paper towels) and dish washing supplies (biodegradable soap or detergent, steel wool pads, nylon scrubber).

Some sort of lantern should live with the kitchen. Many packers use a pressurized white gas lantern or one that operates on bottled gas. White gas lanterns hiss and throw a garish light; bottled gas lanterns just throw a garish light. Smoke, reasoning that quiet and soft light are esthetically valuable and worth packing extra batteries for, prefers a battery powered lantern that can be hung in the kitchen area. For convenience a battery lantern is hard to beat — just turn it on — and unlike either kind of gas lantern, it poses no special packing problems.

Lanterns with glass chimneys and filament mantles need special handling to get from camp to camp intact, and you will have to replace the mantles often. You can buy heavy-duty mantles, and these do seem to be more tolerant of rough handling. Mantles however are cheap and easily replaced. Glass chimneys are neither. There are several ways to protect glass lanterns. The one we use is simply to wrap the lantern in a gunny sack, then roll it in a tent or tarp. The tent provides ample padding, and unless you forget it's in there and kneel directly on it while mantying, the glass will arrive each night intact. As long as the lantern is in good working order, you needn't worry about gas leaking on your tent. The pressure chamber of a white gas lantern is by design as airtight as possible. If yours isn't, the lantern will warn you. It won't hold pressure and the light will fade requiring periodic pumping. Test it before you leave home; if the light fades, replace the rubber gasket inside the filler cap, or replace the cap. If it still fades, the generator may be shot. Silicone spray will prolong the life of rubber seals and will temporarily rejuvenate aged ones.

The other method of packing a lantern

Figure 59.
Stove or campfire?
Just because you enjoy
the radience, warmth and
fellowship of a campfire
doesn't mean you need
to cook over one.

involves building some sort of box to hold it in place. This means one more piece of equipment, but if you pack with soft panyards, it's necessary equipment. We know packers who have built fitted wooden boxes just for lanterns, but a corrugated cardboard box, cut down and reassembled to fit snugly around the lantern works as well and is easier to make. With crumpled newspaper packed around the lantern, these boxes provide good protection.

Packing fuel for lanterns poses additional problems. Gas cartridges are bulky and heavy and they don't get much lighter when empty. White gas is simply hard to pack. The leak-proof gas container hasn't been built, and the problem of gas leaking is exacerbated by changes in altitude and fluctuations in temperature. The gas that just filled the can at 8 a.m. when the temperature was 50 degrees will be fighting to escape by the time you reach that 9,000 foot pass at noon with the temperature up to 75 degrees. Besides being a fire hazard, leaking gas will taint whatever it's packed near, the tent, your jacket, the steaks.

Never pack gas in a glass container. You might as well pack a bomb. In fact, you are packing a bomb, a Molotov cocktail. Gas containers must be metal. The best we know

of are spun aluminum bottles made by Sigg. These are the only containers, except the lantern itself, strong enough and leak-proof enough to pack inside a manty. They are, however, designed for backpackers and hold only a quart, enough for two refills of your lantern.

To carry more, the best container is possibly the can the white gas comes in. The best way to pack this is to put it on the pack saddle between the D-rings and the manties. Bailing twine tied to the handles and then to the D-rings will hold it in place. We use this method when we have to pack a lot of gas into hunting camp.

This is a good time to take up stoves since again the the problem of whether you want to carry gas, or any fuel for that matter, arises. Stoves are a tremendous convenience. They keep the outside of your pots clean, and they make cooking in bad weather much easier — no struggling to light wet wood. But they also add weight to your outfit and pose esthetic and ethical dilemmas.

Gasoline and bottled gas stoves are widely used by backpackers who recognize that heavy backcountry use is depleting firewood supplies and leading to the destruction of live trees near popular campsites. Such stoves with a week's supply of fuel often add less than three pounds to a hiker's load and greatly reduce degradation of the backcountry. Having a single burner is not an inconvenience since backpackers tend to rely on dried foods and to make one-pot stews and casseroles.

There are times when the same reasoning applies to horsepackers. When you pack in to heavily used areas (and this includes most national parks), or you plan to camp in high, fragile alpine areas above timberline, you should feel obligated to carry a stove and fuel. The rest of the time you have a choice: open fire, wood stove, or some type of gas stove.

Do you want a stove at all? A stove is one more piece of equipment, and it can be heavy and bulky. For some people a wood-burning camp stove or a three-burner Coleman smacks too much of civilization's comforts to be welcome in camp. An open fire, casting its circle of light into the surrounding darkness, radiates a warmth that owes nothing to the laws of thermodynamics. We can't argue with any of that.

The strongest argument for stoves is that they make cooking easier. No matter which side of an open fire you sit on, the wind will blow smoke toward you. Stoves let you control both heat intensity and distribution, both crucial if you care enough about your cooking (or eating) to dislike pancakes raw on one edge and burned on the other. Also, by directing heat where you want it, a stove cooks your meals and not your hands. Unless you wear mitts or gloves, a fire usually cooks both.

Just because you want a campfire for atmosphere or evening warmth doesn't mean you have to cook over it. A compromise between a fire and a stove is to carry a sheet of steel to place over your fire rather than the open grate that many people use. The steel will spread the heat, shield your hands from flames and protect your pots.

If you decide you want a stove, you have to choose between wood or gas. The advantages of a gas stove are obvious: you can come into camp, fire it up and be cooking minutes later. That's a break after a long day's ride, particularly when its raining. If that's what you want, and you're willing to pack gasoline or propane bottles, fine. We like wood, largely for esthetic reasons. Wood is traditional and the crackle of a wood stove gives camp a different atmosphere than the hiss of pressurized gas. For fall and early winter hunting camps, a wood stove does double duty; it let's you cook indoors, and it heats your tent. Sure we know about catalytic heaters — more gear. A wood stove gives you something to back up to.

Multiple burner gas and propane camp stoves are available in sporting goods stores and departments, and stores specializing in backpacking equipment carry a wide variety of small backpackers' stoves. Most of these are quite good. A salesman can introduce you to their use and differences.

Figure 60.
Three good
packer's stoves.

a. *The Yukon Stove*

b. *Sims Sportsman*

Wood stoves offer the packer several choices. Cheapest and lightest, at less than 12 pounds, are the sheetmetal airtights. Cheapness and lightness are their only virtues for packing. They dent easily and are hard to cook on. Some packers use barrel stoves, but besides being heavy and awkward to pack, they are really heaters and have to be modified to provide a cooking surface.

Two of the best stoves we know of for small parties are the Sportsman, made by Sims Camp Stoves of Lovell, Wyoming, and the U.S. Army's Yukon stove. Both are efficient, compact and light. The Yukon stove was developed for government use and can be hard to obtain. Usually, it must be purchased as government surplus, but getting one can be worth the trouble. Its packed size, including stove pipe, is 8" x 10" x 24", and it weighs 28 pounds. It is easily included in a mantied load or top packed. The Sportsman is slightly heavier —33 pounds —but it includes an oven and a work counter. Leaving the oven at home reduces the weight to 24 pounds. The Sportsman is, if anything, easier to pack; it folds into a package approximately 24" x 18" x 6", not much larger than a two-burner white-gas stove.

Many packers, Smoke among them, design and redesign their own stoves. They

c. Smoke's Stove

either weld them themselves or have them fabricated by a welding shop. Over the years Smoke has had a succession of similar stoves, each incorporating some slight improvement over its predecessor.

Don't pack your stove empty. Remove the ashes and pack gear in it. The inside of a small stove is a fine place to carry items whose cleanliness isn't critical, such as pickets, bells, shoeing equipment, and stove pipe. Unless both you and your mule are rattleproof, pad everything well. Gunny sacks make good padding and protect things from soot.

Your kitchen should be packed so that everything, including food, is together in one or two locations. An excellent and cheap container for packing kitchen gear is an ordinary cardboard box. The best, if you can get them, are meat or poultry boxes; these are waxed, have handles and tight-fitting lids and are strong enough for 60 t0 70 pound loads. Two make a well shaped manty. Fruit boxes with separate

Figure 61. Waxed meat or chicken boxes are hard to beat for packing food and kitchen gear.

lids that slip completely over the box are also good.

These cardboard boxes can be used to pack all your kitchen equipment and food supplies, including fresh and perishable items. Meat will keep easily for ten days if it is frozen hard before leaving home and handled properly during the trip. Buy only freshly slaughtered meat, meat that has not been hung or previously frozen. Buy your meat at least a week before you leave and keep it in a freezer, set at the lowest temperature possible. You want it just as hard as you can get it. It will help if you have the butcher double wrap the meat for each meal in a single package. With as few packages as possible, surface area and therefore the rate of warming are kept to a minimum. For example, when you have several steaks for one meal, they should be tightly stacked, wrapped and frozen together.

Just before you leave home, wrap each package in several layers of newspaper and pack it in a box reserved for frozen food. Put packages that you will use first around the edges and those will be used later in the trip in the center. A block of dry ice, wrapped in newspaper and packed in the center of the box will keep the packages nearest it frozen perhaps a day or two longer. Dry ice is

expensive and not really necessary unless you're in hot country with warm nights. If there is space remaining in the box, don't fill it with unfrozen items. Instead, fill any empty space with crumpled newspaper.

In camp, keep the meat box, as well as boxes containing perishables like eggs or vegetables, in the shade. Manties — once they have been in the shade awhile themselves — can be piled on these boxes to further insulate them. This is the method Smoke uses on his ten-day summer trips, and even in hot weather meat has not spoiled. We aren't saying that meat will stay frozen this long — it won't — only that it will not spoil. You can also use this method to pack frozen fruit pies.

Eggs present another special problem, and there are several solutions. The first is simply to leave eggs in their cartons. If you're careful, and remember which manty they are in, this works fine. You can improve on this by wrapping each egg in a sheet of tissue paper, then putting it back in the carton. A further refinement is to save empty cartons and use the bottoms to replace the tops of cartons containing eggs, so that there is a molded compartment above and below each egg. The plastic egg containers sold by camping supply stores are a fancier version of this idea, but for

Figure 62a-c. Smoke's kitchen box.

a. Open

b. Packed

horse packing the advantages of these are marginal. They are hardly better than cardboard or styrofoam cartons and you can't — or rather won't — throw them into the fire when they're empty.

Recently, a friend showed us how he breaks every egg into a hollow Tupperware™ rolling pin. This is the ultimate in protective packaging, making it nearly impossible to break a yoke. The narrow mouth lets you dispense eggs one at a time. Although he says he has had no spoilage problems, his method clearly sacrifices the freshness-preserving quality of an intact eggshell. If his idea appeals to you, we suggest you experiment to see how long eggs will keep at home before relying on it during a long trip.

Packing other food items into boxes is straightforward. Just fit everything in so that cans don't crush the bread, and nothing rattles or rolls. You can save a great deal of space and weight, however, if you repackage most processed foods. Coffee and other dry goods are easily transported in doubled plastic freezer bags. Although boxes don't weigh much relative to their contents, repacking boxed foods in freezer bags yields a substantial weight savings, provides better protection against moisture,

c. Padded silverware compartment

and lets you pack more food in less space. When repackaging mixes, tear off the label and directions and include these in each bag. You don't want to confuse powdered milk with soap flakes.

Avoid cans and bottles as much as possible. Not only are they heavy, but you'll have to pack them out. Buy liquids like cooking oil and syrup in plastic containers or rebottle them in leakproof plastic canteens. You can avoid cans almost entirely and eat better at the same time. Although having pack stock frees you from dependence on freeze-dried food, freeze-dried vegetables taste better than canned vegetables at a fraction of their weight and space. There is little reason to carry canned fruit when you can just as easily take fresh fruit.

If you have more than one pack horse, you may want to consider building some sort of kitchen box or boxes. Figure 62 shows Smoke's kitchen box. It is designed to match his stove, making a load of 80 pounds to a side. Like his stove, the kitchen box is manty-size (mantying keeps dust out). The sides fold out to form work counters and, with careful packing, all routine kitchen equipment fits in snugly. Silverware is held in place between layers of compressible foam. Regardless of how you pack your

kitchen, everything should be padded and held securely in place.

Beyond the essentials of a good kitchen, you may appreciate the luxury of a table and folding camp stools. Here again, your age, your string, and your sense of what is appropriate will shape your decision. A table needn't be elaborate. A sheet of plywood 36 x 22 will fit in a manty and can be easily put to use as a table. Strips of lath,

Figure 63a-b. A folding table.

89

b. Table folded.

Tools

During fire season, May 1 through September 30, Montana state law requires all pack strings to have an axe, a shovel and a bucket. There may be a similar law in your state. Even if there isn't, you should carry those three tools. To these add a saw, and you'll have all the heavy machinery you need.

Tools are best carried outside your manties where you can get at them easily. Axes and shovels can be laced through manty ropes (Figure 65) or they can be hung beneath loads (Figure 66). Our axe and shovel guards have a strap that buckles around the front D-ring. Handles are then lassoed with one of the loops of sling rope on the rear D-ring. All bladed tools, axe,

linked side by side like a snow fence, make a table top that can be rolled up but is very solid when unrolled along two parallel poles. Many local packers use a folding table with built-in seats made by the Milwaukee Stamping Co. that weighs 35 pounds and folds to 34 x 4 x 15 (Figure 63).

Figure 64. Essential tools – shovel, saw and axe. All blades should have covers.

90

Figure 65. Axe through manty ropes.

Figure 66a-c. Shovel, saw, and axe hung from D-rings. These ride under the loads.

shovel and saw, should have guards or covers. Effective saw guards can be made by cutting a groove in a strip of lumber or splitting open a length of canvas firehose, fitting this over the saw teeth, and tying it in place.

We prefer a double bitted axe. Having two blades let's us use one edge — marked with paint — for all wood splitting. The other blade is kept very sharp and used only for clearing trail. If double bits scare you or you doubt your ability to use one safely, stick to a single bit. You may want to carry a pulaski, which gives you an extra tool, a mattock, without adding much weight. Whatever you choose, get a full length handle. For an adult, it will be safer and easier on your back than a three-quarter length. For the same reason, you want a shovel with at least a 36 inch handle. Entrenching tools are for the infantry; you've got a mule to carry your shovel.

Smoke's saw is half of a two-man crosscut, but most people carry bowsaws. Bowsaws come in a great variety of sizes and designs, but besides a sharp blade, the only important consideration is that the bow be deep enough to let you cut something besides twigs.

Figure 67.
Collapsable
plastic buckets.

Plastic buckets are light and quiet, but collapsible canvas buckets are more rugged, easier to pack, and they also keep water cooler. Buckets can be mantied, but tying them to the front D-ring keeps them handy and lets you keep them out as you break camp.

You'll also need some smaller tools for minor repairs. A good tool kit which can conveniently live with the kitchen includes a screwdriver, a pliers, a bastard file, a sewing kit and stitching awl, a roll of duct tape, and a flashlight. There's no need to carry extra rope or pieces of leather. By using longer latigos than necessary, you'll have some you can cut off, and our recommended lengths for sling ropes also give you extra.

We're going to stretch a point and include first-aid kits under tools. You'll need one, and you'll have a better one if you put it together yourself rather than buying a pre-assembled kit. The following list is prepared for a small group of horsemen planning to stay in the backcountry for two weeks or less. We are assuming there are no medically-knowledgeable persons such as doctors or nurses along. All of the items on the basic list can be purchased in a drug store without a prescription. An optional list contains suggestions for more sophisticated medical gear.

First-aid Kit

Basic Kit

Sterile gauze — 4" x 4" pads — 1-2 packs
Telfa® pads — 8" x 3" size, 3" x 4" size — a few of each
Band-Aids®
Adhesive tape — 1" wide
Paper tape — 1" wide
Soap
Iodine solution
Triangular sling
Ace bandages — 4" — 2
Eye patches — a few for scratches on cornea)
Moleskin® — for blisters
Neosporin ointment
Q-Tips® — for removing foreign object from eye or wound
Aspirin and Tylenol®
Snakebite kit
Sunscreen containing DABA

Optional Kit

Anakit® — contains injectable epinephrine (adrenalin) and antihistamine tablets for severe allergic reactions
Squeeze bottle for washing wounds & eyes — boil water & bottle
Steri-strips® — to close wounds on the face
Finger splint — metal or use tongue depressors
Cotton padding
Thermometer
Sterile needle — removing slivers
Suture set — xylocaine, needle holder, suture material
Inflatable splints — 2, 1 arm& 1 leg

Prescription Drugs

Those with chronic or recurrent diseases such as asthma, bladder infections, diabetes, or allergies should consult their physicians and consider bringing an emergency supply of medication along. Sterile Bullet® — or other suitable anesthetics

If you don't know first-aid, learn it. In most cities, the American Red Cross offers courses in basic first-aid on a regular basis. Your kit won't do you much good in an emergency if you don't know how to use it.

Many people who wouldn't dream of leaving civilization without a first-aid kit ride blithely into the hills without a thought about what they'd do if a horse were injured. You need a horse first-aid kit too.

Horse & Mule First-aid Kit

Granulex® or scarlet oil
Pytenol lotion or blue lotion
Nitrofurazone soluble dressing or Demafur®
Sulfa-urea powder
Blood-stop Powder®
Hydrogen peroxide
Absorbine®
Cotton
Gauze bandages
Ace bandages
Thermometer

These are aerosols, ointments, and powders useful for common horse injuries and available in pharmacies that handle veterinary supplies. They are only a few of the many that might be used. Your vet may suggest others. This particular list, however, has proven its value on our horses and mules in the field.

Remember that any injury below the knee is potentially very serious. There is little muscle tissue in this area; the blood supply is limited; it is in continual motion which tends to aggravate injuries; and because it is close to the ground, it is hard to keep clean, increasing the chances of infection. Injuries above the knee can generally be treated differently because they involve muscle tissue and a good blood supply. Here are some of the treatments we have found to be sound and easily administered:

Conditions Above The Knee

Earmites/sore ears causes head-shyness and tenderness of the ears. Treat with a few drops of warm olive oil on cotton, rubbed or daubed in the ear.

Deep muscle cuts and punctures. When there is an open wound with bleeding, use Blood Stop Powder®, covering the area thoroughly. In the absence of heavy bleeding, scarlet oil or Granulex® — both of which stimulate tissue growth — may be used. Neither should ever be applied below the knee, however, since they can cause proud flesh on unmuscled areas. One of the antibiotic agents — nitrofurazone, Demafur® or sulfa urea powder — will

Figure 68. Easy Boot.

lessen the chances of infection. Use whichever is easiest to apply.

Saddle sores, abrasions, cinch sores, rope burns and wire cuts. The following are all excellent: nitrofurazone soluble dressing; pytenol lotion; and blue lotion.

To clean a wound use a solution of hydrogen peroxide.

Mange or loss of hair. A wash with solution of one part Chlorox® to ten parts water helps. This is also good for ringworm. To recover the horse's natural hair color on a wounded area, apply a solution of alum powder and water as the new hair grows over the healed wound. This will not be 100 percent successful on all horses.

Conditions Below The Knee

Lameness due to bowed tendons, sore ligaments or sore tendons. Rub down the affected area with Absorbine® several times a day. Rest the horse. Horses with bowed tendons should not be worked.

Injuries to the coronet band and hoof. Apply nitrofurazone soluble dressing or Dermafur dressing. Cracks in the hoof can be treated with pine tar. Cracks causing lameness may have to be immobilized by your farrier with a special shoe.

Nail punctures and frog injuries. Thoroughly clean the area with hydrogen peroxide or a solution of chlorox and water in equal amounts.

When applied to serious injuries in the hills, these treatments are first-aid only. Consult your vet as soon as possible.

The most common horse or mule problem is thrown shoes, and you should have some equipment to deal with this when it arises. Replacing a shoe isn't difficult, if you know what you're doing, and if your horse or mule will stand to be shod. Ask your farrier for some lessons the next time he shoes your stock. In the backcountry, you'll want to carry a spare shoe in each of the sizes required by your animals, some shoeing nails, a rasp and a light hammer, or a pair of fencing pliers. You can clinch nails against the edge of the rasp.

If your mule can't be shod standing, if you aren't comfortable working on your horse's feet, or if there is any doubt in your mind about your ability to put on a shoe correctly, there's an alternative — a rubber boot called Easy Boot™ (Figure 68). This slips on over the hoof and clamps tight with a ski boot buckle. These boots are easy to use and remarkably durable, though they slosh after stream crossings. They are also a safe solution to the problem of mules who won't stand to to be shod.

Personal Gear

The following equipment lists were developed from checklists Smoke sends to people booking trips with him. These recommendations have been developed over 15 years and have worked out well. If you're already an experienced camper, you'll know what you want to take for different seasons. But if you're just beginning, this is a good starting point.

SUMMER/EARLY FALL

Equipment
Sleeping bag — 2⅓-3 lb. down or equivalent
   synthetic insulation
Fishing tackle and license
Camera and film
Flashlight & extra batteries
Knife
Maps and compass

Clothing
Poncho or slicker
Warm jacket
Sweater — optional
Riding boots
Camp shoes — tennis shoes or moccasins
Hat — broad brimmed felt or straw
Blue jeans — 2 pair
Cotton shirts — 2-3 long sleeved
Underwear
Long johns — optional
Warm up suit — for sleeping
Socks — 3 pair, 1 pair wool
Gloves — light leather or leather palm

Incidentals
Insect repellant
Sun lotion
Soap
Kleenex or toilet tissue
Towel and wash cloth
Toothbrush & toothpaste
Other toiletries
Drinking cup
Matches in waterproof container

HUNTING SEASON/WINTER

Add or substitute

Rifle, ammunition, license
Binoculars

Hunting knife

Snow pacs
Hat with ear flaps
Wool pants — 1 pair
Wool shirts

Long underwear

Socks — 3 pair wool, 3 pair lighter
Extra pair warm gloves or mittens

Chapstick

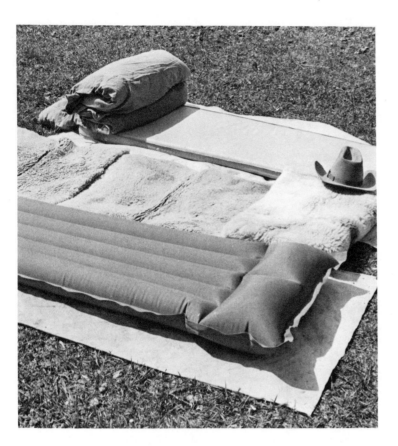

Figure 69. Three mattresses – (top to bottom) foam pad, saddle pads, and air mattress.

A good sleeping bag is the most important item of personal equipment. One third of your pack trip will be spent sleeping, or shivering and trying to. For summer and early fall in the Northern Rockies, you want a sleeping bag designed to be comfortable to 10°F. You can expect to pay $80 to $100 for a bag stuffed with one of the good synthetic fills like Hollofil II® or Polarguard®. Comparable goose down-filled bags are slightly lighter, more compressible and more durable, but cost between 50 and 100 percent more. All other things being equal, a mummy style bag will be warmer. The difference will be most noticeable if you sleep outside a tent when there's a breeze. Sleeping bag covers and liners improve the insulation value of any bag and make it easier to keep clean.

No matter how good your sleeping bag, you need a mattress, not because the ground is often hard and lumpy, but because it's cold. The highly compressible insulation used in sleeping bags flattens under your body weight and becomes very ineffective. The most commonly used types of mattresses are air mattresses or foam pads. The pine-bough bed is very destructive and neither of us finds air mattresses very comfortable. They aren't particularly good insulators and sooner or later even the best leak. If you like air mattresses, spend a few extra dollars and get one made of heavier fabric-backed material.

Foam pads come in two styles, open and closed cell foam. Closed cell pads are light, excellent insulators and won't absorb water. They are, however, thin, three-eighths to half an inch, and therefore fairly hard. Pads of open cell foam offer the best combination of cushioning and warmth, but they are bulky. If they get wet, they will soak up water like a sponge and are impossible to wring out. If an open cell pad is in contact with water, it will wick the moisture through to your sleeping bag. Unless the next day is hot and dry, you'll spend more than one wet, uncomfortable night. Don't buy an open cell pad that doesn't have a waterproof cover.

Packers, however, don't need to carry a special mattress at all. If you use synthetic fleece saddle pads, you already own the most comfortable backcountry bed we've ever slept on. You've got to keep them clean, though, and clean side up unless you don't mind your sleeping bag smelling like essence of sweaty horse.

As a minimum, you'll want one complete change of clothes and you'll do less washing if you take at least two changes of underwear and socks. For use around camp, you may want shoes other than your riding boots.

Periodic bad weather is a fact of life in the mountains. It can snow in any month. Even in July, you may need cold and wet weather gear. A light down jacket packs easily and will ward off any summer cold snap. As fall approaches, add long underwear and a wool shirt or sweater. By late fall, you should be relying on wool and down or the downlike synthetics for your outer clothes. Nothing equals wool's ability to conserve heat, even when wet.

Because you may have to wear rain gear in the saddle, the best alternatives are the traditional cowboy slicker, split fore and aft to hang over the horse, or a hip length rain jacket worn with rain pants. A Gore-Tex® parka will double as a light jacket and a raincoat. Chaps, given a generous treatment of wax-based waterproofing (or even floor wax) make acceptable rain pants. Smooth leather chaps waterproof better than roughout. For use around camp, the rainsuit, jacket and pants, is probably more convenient than the slicker. Smoke prefers this combination. Don't forget a plastic hat cover. Western straw hats don't keep out rain, and after an hour or so of steady rain, they'll be drooping down around your chin. Rubber boots, the style that will go over your riding boots, are a nice extra even when the weather is dry, since walking

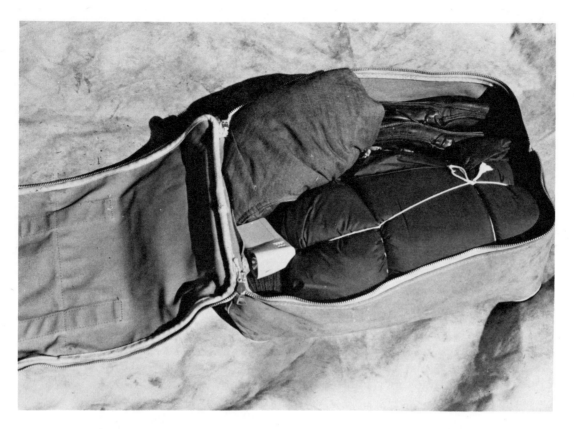

Figure 70.
Smoke packs all
his personal gear
in this small
duffle bag.

through a dew-drenched meadow can leave leather boots soaked for the rest of the day.

Unless you want to cultivate a mountain-man image, you'll need your razor, shaving cream, toothbrush, toothpaste, soap, towel and anything else you must have to keep yourself feeling presentable. Leave non-essential cosmetics home, particularly scents and aftershaves. It won't hurt you to smell like a person for a week, and you'll be less likely to wake up with a bear licking your face.

Packing personal gear in a small to medium duffle bag makes it easy to manty. If you organize duffle in small plastic bags, socks in one bag, underwear in another, you won't have to dump everything out to find your spare handkerchief, and the plastic bags add protection against rain and snow. Items that you'll want during the day, binoculars, camera, notebook, insect repellant, toilet paper, raingear, go on your saddle or in your saddle bags. That's too

much already. If you can't restrain yourself, a ditty bag hung from the saddle horn is easier on your horse than bulging saddle bags.

Summary

The only sweeping generalization we can make about camps is that every packer assembles his own. There is no perfect camp. Although we've tried to single out the basics, we recognize that what's indispensable to one packer is fluff to another. This is partly because we all tend to confuse equipment with the function it serves. As you choose equipment, keep in mind the job it's meant to do. Ask yourself: Does each item do an essential job? Will something you already have in your outfit do as well?

We've told you to travel light, but also to take what you need to be comfortable. We can't resolve the contradiction in this

advice because no two of us are going to agree exactly on what's light and where minimal comfort begins and ends.

In *These Thousand Hills*, A.B. Guthrie's novel of the cowboy era in Montana, an old trailboss was fond of saying "...tastes got a right to diffeh." We agree. Within reason, you should decide what kind of camp you're going to run. As a rough rule of thumb, the bounds of reason can be defined in terms of the size of a pack string. A camp that requires between one pack animal per rider and one pack animal per two riders is a reasonable camp. Within those limits, what you take is up to you, and whether you pack a table or not is nobody's business but yours.

Appendix I lists the contents of a camp for four people including food for an eight-day trip and shows you how to arrange it so it will go on three pack animals — two if you don't pack feed. This is offered primarily as a starting point if you have never packed or camped. For those who have, it can be an aid to memory, planning and packing. From it you can build the camp you want, and you can vary your camp from trip to trip, season to season. After a few trips, you should review the contents of your outfit to see if there are items you never use. If there are, and they're not essentials for an emergency — like your first-aid kit — leave them out. Adding items is easy. Resist that urge and try to select gear that will serve several uses.

*Figure 71. Where the family car is a pickup, a
horse trailer may be the most economical way to
haul your horses, but a light truck won't haul a
very large trailer safely.*

chapter six
Gas Burners For Hayburners

Nice as it would be to saddle your string behind the barn, ride down the driveway and disappear into the hills, reality for most of us involves shipping horses to a trailhead. Recreational packers are more likely to live at the edge of a subdivision than the edge of the wilderness.

Shipping horses is a skill in its own right. There are as many ways to screw up between home and the trailhead as there are once you're in the saddle. It's not enough for a modern packer to know horses and hitches; he has to know something about stock vehicles and how to use them. A mechanized skill has been grafted onto a non-mechanized tradition.

Trucks & Trailers

To ship horses and mules, you'll need either a trailer or a stock truck. Trailers are the most popular, though we doubt that this is due to any intrinsic superiority. For most people, trailers are simply the most economical alternative. Here in the West, the family car is often a pickup truck. Where owning a stock truck means a second vehicle with limited usefulness, a comparable trailer usually costs less and the family pickup is already there to pull it.

Also many people feel more comfortable pulling a trailer than driving a large truck. A trailer leaves them behind the wheel of a familiar vehicle. It stops and starts slower, but otherwise it handles normally. Don't be lulled by the sense of security you get when a trailer is towing well under good conditions. It takes considerably more skill than most of us possess to handle a truck and trailer rig in an emergency. If either the truck or the trailer starts to slide, you're suddenly riding a horse with two heads. If you're only hauling two horses, a trailer is fine. But high winds, long winding hills and icy roads bring out the hidden drawbacks of many larger trailers.

Light-duty trucks with bumper-mounted hitches don't mix well with large trailers. Look at Figure 71. Depending on size, design and load distribution, one-third to one-half of a trailer's weight rides on the rear bumper of the towing truck, a point well behind the rear wheels. Some of this weight is carried by the rear suspension, but the rear axle also acts like a fulcrum, the pivot of a seesaw, levering weight off the truck's front wheels and reducing control.

You don't believe us? Your truck's a three-quarter ton and it never handles better than when you've got three quarters of a ton

Figure 72.
This trailer
holds six horses
or mules, loaded
three abreast.
It is large for
a straight-neck trailer
but it is always
towed with a
one-ton truck.

in the bed. We won't argue with that, but that three-quarters of a ton is spread over the whole bed, not just over the rear bumper. Put it behind the axle and see how your truck steers on a slick road.

A loaded four-horse trailer can equal, or exceed the weight of some light-duty trucks. If that trailer blows a tire or starts to slide on an icy road, it can end up towing your truck. For safety with a bumper hitch, truck weight should exceed trailer weight by one-third.

If you want and need a bigger trailer, the solution isn't a bigger truck; it's a goose-neck trailer. The gooseneck design distributes the weight of the trailer over the rear wheels. This mimics the weight arrangement of long-haul, fifth wheelers giving a goose-neck excellent handling characteristics. The truck's suspension dampens side to side wobble. The trailer tows truer, turns tighter and backs easier. And the front wheels of your truck stay firmly on the road. This better weight

distribution carries one slight drawback — a gooseneck may be somewhat harder to tow in snow. This is minor. People who regularly haul large strings — ten or more head — with gooseneck trailers and pickups, swear by these rigs.

Brakes are an area where nearly all trailers fall short. Trailer brakes are usually electric brakes. When activated by the brake pedal, an electromagnet moves an eccentric cam that forces the brake shoe against the drum. Unlike car brakes, stopping pressure isn't controlled by the pressure of your foot. Electric brakes are an all-or-nothing proposition. They have to be adjusted so that they won't lock and so they apply equal pressure to both sides of the trailer. This is easier said than done, and ice, water, rust and dirt work relentlessly to upset this fine balance. Electric brakes are also only as good as the electrical hookup between truck and trailer. You should check the wiring harness for broken wires each time you plug it in. Then check the trailer brake operation

Figure 73.
A gooseneck trailer
is better for large
loads of horses.
Notice the ribs
over the trailer.
In cold weather,
it can be fitted
with a canvas top.

This combination
would be safer if the
truck had dual rear tires.
Harley Hettick

before you're on the highway. To do this, you need a manual brake-control lever in the cab allowing you to activate the trailer's brakes independently of the truck's. If the brakes are working, you'll feel the trailer hanging back.

Even though they can create problems, you need trailer brakes. They keep the trailer from passing you when you have to stop faster than you or your stock would like, and they reduce the risk of brake fade from overheated truck brakes on long downgrades. Tandem-wheeled trailers come with either two- or four-wheel brakes. Four sounds twice as good as two, so many people order four-wheel brakes. Yet four-wheel brakes are actually more dangerous. With two-wheel brakes, if one wheel locks on an icy road, you still have one free-rolling wheel on that side trying to keep the trailer running in a straight line. With four-wheel brakes, locking up one side can throw you into the ditch or an oncoming car.

There are times when you may not want your trailer brakes at all, so it's a good idea to have a switch in the cab that lets you turn them off. On curving, slippery downgrades where you're going to be on and off your brakes for miles, you can gear down and rely on compression and your truck's brakes while the trailer's wheels keep it on the road. Of course, your truck had better have good brakes.

Some trailers come equipped with hydraulic surge brakes. A hydraulic cylinder, mounted on the hitch, links the trailer brake with the body of the truck. Whenever the truck stops or slows, the trailer rides forward, the cylinder is compressed and the brakes go on. This might be a good idea on the plains, but its terrible in the mountains. On downgrades, your trailer brakes are on constantly. Overheated brakes do nothing but wear out fast.

Hitches are one more place for things to go wrong with disasterous results. With the

Figure 74.
This one-ton stock truck
is an excellent vehicle
for recreational packers.
With its ten-foot bed
it will carry four
large horses or mules
easily — five with a
good last loader.

older cup and ball hitches, it is possible to tow a trailer even though the hitch isn't locked. If you have this type, you should check it carefully and often. Newer trailers are equipped with hitches that lock from the side. With these, you can't move the trailer an inch unless the hitch is locked. Dropping a trailer in the driveway is preferable to having it come off while you're bouncing down some dirt road or doing 50 on the interstate.

Generally we prefer stock trucks to trailers because we think they are safer. A truck brakes truer and handles more predictably. Because there's only one unit, and you're in it, you feel instantly everything that goes on: sways, skids, or a wheel off the shoulder. You also have a feel for what is happening among your horses and mules. If a horse is acting up or in trouble, you know it immediately. With a large trailer, big problems can go undetected for miles.

A stock truck also carries your animals at

right angles to the line of travel. This is safe, and the only good way to load stock on a truck. Horses and mules, with little room to move, balance well from front to back but badly from side to side. Loaded across the truck, they can deal with curves (which are unavoidable), and you can help them with their side-to-side balance by stopping and starting gradually. Alternating animals head-to-tail discourages fighting and makes the most complete use of the truck's floor space. It also reduces the danger of horses stepping on and cutting each other since their feet are staggered.

Trailers, in which horses are hauled parallel to the direction of travel, need dividers to support horses on curves, keep down fighting and prevent cut ankles. The safest arrangement in undivided trailers is to place horses diagonally. If the trailer is wide enough to turn a horse around in, horses can even be staggered head to tail. The diagonal arrangement wastes space, but for balance, it is even better than

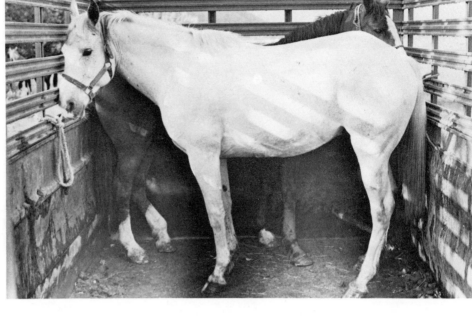

*Figure 75.
Stock loaded
across a truck
can brace against
side-to-side sway.
Staggered head-to-tail,
they are less likely
to step on each other.*

Harley Hettick

loading across a truck.

Stock trucks do have disadvantages. The most dangerous is that they are top heavy. A high center of gravity, raised higher yet by a load of horses, makes them easy to roll over. To load or unload most trucks, you need a loading ramp or a dirt embankment of the right height, and unloading along the highway in an emergency can be a problem. We've already mentioned the greater cost of trucks than comparable trailers. To that add higher taxes, insurance and licensing costs.

Safety & Comfort

Whether you ship by truck or trailer, you owe your stock a safe, comfortable ride. Besides humanitarian considerations, your animal will load better and ride more quietly if travel isn't a traumatic experience. Safety and comfort are your responsibility. You can buy vehicles with good features; you can improve most vehicles yourself; and you can drive with

consideration for your stock.

Have enough room for each horse or mule. Some two-horse trailers are too short or too low, some stock trucks too narrow. An average horse or mule needs seven feet of length and at least two feet of width.

Next put yourself in your horse's place — literally. If you have a trailer — or a truck, for that matter, though trailers are usually worse — have a friend drive it down a dirt road with you in the back. When your ears stop ringing, do something about the noise. Glue carpet or spray undercoating under the metal roof. Canvas topped trucks and trailers are quieter. At high speeds, wind adds to the noise, and in winter wind, you can make life intolerably cold for the first horses in a load. The front of stock racks and trailers should be screened against the wind.

On the road, balance is your stock's biggest problem. They need good footing. The rubber door mats that cover the floor in some trailers help, but they are also one

Figure 76.
The back edge
of a trailer
should be rounded.

more thing for animals to get tangled in. Remember Murphy's Law: "Whatever can go wrong...." We shovel a layer of sand or fine gravel over the wood floor. Don't use shavings, chips or straw. These can be very slippery.

Before you cover the floor, give some thought to its durability. No one ever looks at the floor of a truck or trailer; it's always covered with manure. Floors take a beating from stamping, urine and manure, and in time, even the best floors will rot out or wear out. You don't want a horse sticking a foot through the floor. We cover floors with plywood. It's relatively cheap and easy to replace. At the same time, sheathing the bottom three feet of the walls with plywood or conveyor belting will reduce wear and tear on the vehicle and keep down noise. Some animals will kick metal walls just to annoy you. Hobble them.

Go looking for sharp edges and protrusions, anything that a horse or mule can cut or impale himself on. Murphy's law

again. A common trouble spot is the back edge of the floor on trailers. An animal backing off is likely to be surprised by the step down and will often step under the trailer as his foot goes to the ground. Even a wide undivided trailer, allowing stock to be turned around and led out, should have a smooth lip at the back. Again and again we have seen horses, who should know better, step off the end as if it were level with the ground. Maybe coming into the light, they don't see well. Whatever the reason, tendons can be bruised scraping across a sharp edge. Rubber padding or a round pipe welded to the edge will prevent injuries.

Your stock will ride more quietly at night if there is a light on in the trailer or stock rack to shield them from the glare of oncoming headlights. Instead of shifting patterns of light and dark, your animals will see each other and familiar surroundings. If you have to untangle horses in the dark, having a light beats working with a flashlight in your mouth.

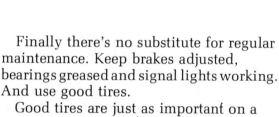

Figure 77.
There should be
no gap between
the back of a truck
and the loading
dock or embankment.
Harley Hettick

Finally there's no substitute for regular maintenance. Keep brakes adjusted, bearings greased and signal lights working. And use good tires.

Good tires are just as important on a trailer as on a truck. Some people run their trailers on bald tires for years. But then some people who disarm bombs for a living live to retire too. When you're towing expensive livestock, worn tires are poor economy. There's a lot of strain on trailer tires and more sway than you feel in your pickup. When the roads are slippery, tread keeps the trailer trailing.

Loading and Unloading

Loading shouldn't become an occasion to abuse horses or mules. The time to train your animals to load is long before you want to go somewhere.

There are uncounted ways to force an unwilling horse or mule onto a truck or trailer. Most aren't very subtle and rely on force or intimidation. That these work only proves what everyone already knows — horses may be stronger, but men are smarter. Stubbornness is a tossup. With enough perseverance, you can get any horse

or mule who ever lived on a truck or trailer, but don't imagine for a moment that you've begun to teach that animal to load. You're more likely to have done the opposite. We aren't going to show you any of these methods. There's no shortage of horsemen who will gladly demonstrate their favorite fool-proof method loading reluctant stock.

When a horse or mule won't go into a trailer or truck, it's either because the experience is new, and he doesn't trust you enough to follow you in, or because he's been in one of those things before and didn't like it. If you start beating, yelling and otherwise coercing him, you're only

107

Figure 78.
*The horse in
this picture is
more experienced
than the handler.
The girl is pulling
on the lead rope,
but this old horse
has unloaded too
many times to let
himself be rushed.*
Harley Hettick

confirming what's already in his head —
that this contraption isn't any place for a
nice critter like him.

Training an animal to load and keeping
him trained are two different things. First
you have to overcome his initial fear of
something new — the truck or trailer. Then
you have to keep him unafraid by always
giving him a good ride. Some young horses
and mules will follow you or another horse
into a vehicle on the first try. If yours won't
load after one or two tries without
becoming excited, don't force the issue.
You don't want him to get the idea that this
is a time he can successfully defy you. End
the lesson, and the next morning serve

breakfast inside. Put grain or pellets just out
of reach in the vehicle and make sure he
knows they're there. Tie back the door and
anything else he might tangle with, and
leave him alone to contemplate the
alternatives — get in or go hungry. After a
week of eating in the truck he should be
eager to get in. To keep him that way,
always give him a comfortable ride, door to
door.

Load and unload carefully. Have solid
footing at both your loading and unloading
point. With a truck you'll need a loading
dock, a portable ramp or a roadside
embankment. Avoid locations that involve
a step of more than a foot or so up or down
and be sure there is no gap between the back
of the truck and the ramp. If there's a hole,
some horse is going to find it and stick a foot
through it.

Don't rush him as he gets in or out. Give
him time to look at his footing or feel his
way, but speak his name so that he's paying
attention. A loose lead is best unless the
animal exploits it to balk at loading. You'll
have better success with many horses and
mules if you don't face them head on. Most
lead better when your back is toward them.
You can watch their progress over your
shoulder.

On the truck, tie each animal short with a quick release knot about chin high. Tying stock is discussed at the start of the next chapter. Tie every animal. If you put a loose horse at the back of a load, he'll just have to see what the front looks like, and he'll wreak havoc getting there. Don't hesitate to rope off trouble makers to keep them in place. Some big horses like to push other horses and mules around. If you let them, they'll crowd everyone into one end of the truck.

Give some thought to the order of loading. You want horses that get along well next to each other. Mules rarely fight. The order in which your string travels down the trail is generally a good one, though there are often reasons to alter it. Don't put two mares next to each other. They'll nip and bicker the entire trip. Also, your first and last horses should be fool-proof loaders. Good last loaders are real prizes because they can stretch the capacity of your truck. Generally last loaders are smaller, supple horses with a special talent for tucking their hindquarters in the door as they turn sideways into the narrow space remaining at the back of a truck. Loading the last horse is the one time you may want to have a helper physically assist a horse. Many last loaders depend on a well-timed push from a handler to get their hindquarters in and around.

Besides being an easy loader, the first horse or mule on a truck should be one of your larger animals. Place him with his tail toward the center of the road. He won't be facing oncoming headlights, but more importantly, you've unbalanced the truck slightly to the inside. If you continue by loading your other heavy horses in the odd spaces — third, fifth, etc. — where they face the side of the road, the inside of the truck will be heavier, and the truck will be more stable if the road is improperly banked or if an outside wheel drops off the pavement into the shoulder.

The Law

The stock rustler did not pass into history with the open range and the cowboy. In most western states laws that make you subject to arrest for horse theft, a felony, if you cross county lines without a valid brand inspection, are a living legacy of the old west. Few recreational horsemen are aware of these laws and countless pillars-of-the-community become desperate lawbreakers each weekend as they head to the mountains with their horses and mules in tow.

A brand inspection is a piece of paper, similar to a certificate of title to your car, that says you own a horse or mule. You need one for each animal, even those that aren't branded. In Montana, brand inspections are issued by the state brand inspector's office and cost a dollar a head per year. Lifetime inspections are available for five dollars.

You can also run afoul of the law if you cross state lines without a health certificate for your stock. Your veterinarian will know what tests are required for your state of destination. Health regulations are set by the federal government, not the states, and are updated monthly. Some tests require several days to complete laboratory analysis, so you should apply for a health certificate at least a week before your planned departure.

For travel to Mexico or Canada, the health certificate must be approved by a district federal veterinarian. It is sometimes possible to secure this approval at heavily used border stations, but not all stations have veterinary officers, and even if they do, should you wish to cross at night, you will have to wait until morning. You will eliminate considerable uncertainty if you get your health certificate approved in advance.

Crossing state lines with your truck or trailer can also lead you into a morass of regulations and permit requirements. The fact that you're on your vacation and didn't know that you needed to apply for reciprocity for your truck or an interstate truck permit isn't going to impress weigh station attendants or state troopers. Write ahead to the states you're going to enter, and find out what documentation your vehicles require.

With that, having paid our respect to the bureaucracy we're trying to leave behind, we can get back to the important business of riding through the hills....

*North Fork
of the Blackfoot,
Scapegoat Wilderness.*
Harley Hettick

chapter seven
Hitting The Trail

You are now on the verge of beginning what this book is all about, riding mountain trails. You're at the trailhead. Your horses and mules are unloaded and tied, preferably to your truck, a hitching rack or a picket line rather than trees. Before you can mount up and head out, you face the logistical problems of loading and assembling your string.

The first thing you want to do is saddle all your stock. Leave the girths just tight enough to keep the saddles from slipping and retie each animal. Letting horses and mules stand saddled doesn't burden them much, and it warms their backs and lets them shake their saddles down into a comfortable position.

A word on tying horses or mules. In the course of a packing season, we see guests tying horses in every way imaginable except the right one. Many of these people have horses of their own and should know better. Here we are going to abandon tolerance and maintain that there is only one right way to tie horses and an infinite number of wrong ways. There is very little middle ground.

There are four ways to go wrong tying horses and mules: tying with the wrong thing; tying with an unsuitable knot; tying too low; or tying too long. Reins are for controlling a horse when you're on his back; halters and lead ropes are for tying up. The proper height for your knot is chin high or slightly higher when the animal is standing in a normal, relaxed position. The

Figure 79a-c. Tie-up knot.

a.

b.

tying to trees, posts or hitch rails. It will tend to slip down smooth posts and tree trunks, but this problem can be overcome by taking two wraps around the post before tying the knot. Because these knots are easily untied, some animals learn to untie themselves. You can usually foil such characters by loosely threading the jerk end of the rope through the loop in the knot.

We don't like to saddle or bridle horses while they're tied, but like everyone else, we're often lazy and do it anyway. With most horses this poses no problems. Sooner or later, though, a nervous horse will object to you ducking under the rope, tightening the cinch or bending his ear to put on the bridle, and he'll pull back violently. If you act quickly, pulling on the quick release knot he's tied with, you can turn him loose, and that will usually end the hysterics. But there's always a chance that you'll be injured by a lunging, pulling horse. If the saddle slips under an already excited animal or a halter breaks, a bad situation can rapidly get worse. I've known one horse, a chronic, unregenerate puller, who finally killed himself when he broke a halter rope and went over backward. Tying a horse short and high seems to deter some pullers, but its no substitute for strong halters and nylon lead ropes without snaps.

proper rope length between the halter and the knot is the distance from the ground to the horse's or mule's chin in the same position. A suitable knot is, first, one that you can untie simply by pulling the jerk-end of the rope. Second, it must be secure enough that an animal tied for hours at a time can't get loose. And third, you should be able to untie it easily even after a 1000 pound horse has pulled against it.

The knot we feel best meets these criteria is illustrated in Figure 79. We use it for

c.

The saddle horse who can break undamaged half-inch nylon hasn't been born. A mule that habitually pulls back is rare.

If you mantied all your gear at home, you're ready to start loading. If you didn't, now is the time. Manty loads in pairs, and when you're done, heft both to see if they're the same. With a little practice, your aching back can become an amazingly accurate scale. If there is a discernable difference, the loads are more than the permissible five pounds apart, and you'll have to open one and add or subtract something. When they're balanced, lean one against the other to keep the pairs together. Remember which are your heaviest loads — often not the biggest — so you can put them on your bigger, stronger animals. Also remember which manties contain breakables like eggs, so these can be loaded on particularly reliable animals.

Before you begin loading your stock, park your vehicles properly. Move them so that they don't block the road or the loading area. If you have more than one vehicle, leave 20 feet between them. The Forest Service likes this spacing so they can get around them with fire fighting gear, and if a shorted wire causes a fire in one, the others won't burn too. Lock up everything that will lock. It's a sad commentary on our society, but trailheads are a setup for vandals and thieves. Last summer we returned from a two-week trip to find the gas syphoned out of the truck's auxiliary tank.

Loading is easier if you lead Mohammed (that's the big mule with a blaze like an oil derrick) to the mountain. Position him between his two manties or panyards. Tie him or have a partner hold him. There are few predicaments in life more frustrating than trying to land a 100-pound manty on a mule who's wandering around trying to eat. Remember to match weight and contents to the animal's size and personality, and remember to cinch up before you put on that first load. An assistant also helps if you have round-backed, fat or low-withered pack stock. One of you can support the unbalanced load while the other gets its mate in place. If you're alone, don't waste any time getting that second manty on the Decker. It doesn't take long for a single manty or panyard to slip under a mule's belly where it's likely to be kicked into the middle of next week.

Take time to balance each pair of loads after it's on the mule. It's easier and in the

*Figure 80.
Clearing trail.
Early in the season,
you'll have to do it,
and you'll get the
job done quicker if
your tools are packed
on the lead mule
where you can get them
more easily.*
Harley Hettick

The right way to shift a load is to change the position where the sling rope encircles the manty. Don't just pull a load down and away from the D-rings. Regardless of how high or low you position a load, it should be snugged up to within an inch of the D-rings. When you think a pair of loads is balanced, check it one last time. For this final check, I like to rock the loads very gently with only the pressure of one or two fingers. I think I can feel the balance or lack of it as well as I can see it in the D-rings.

Trail working equipment, saws, axes and shovels, go outside of your loads where you can get at them without undoing everything. They're handy for balancing loads that you didn't get quite right, but if you have a choice, load them on a mule or horse at the front of the string where you can get at them quickly to cut through deadfall that you can't get around.

By loading your pack string in the order it goes down the trail, you can assemble the string as each animal is loaded. After the first mule is loaded, tie her up. When the second mule is ready, tie her to the pigtail of the first and so on. If, however, your string is fresh, restless or inexperienced, you may want to forego this efficiency and wait until all the stock is loaded before tying them together.

We pigtail all our pack stock. Pigtailing is a system of tying mules and horses together

long run faster, to get the balance right in camp or at the trailhead than it is once you're underway. Even two perfectly equal manties may not balance in the first positions you try. With the loads basket-hitched in place, rock them vigorously from side to side. Let go, and see where they come to rest. The D-rings should center perfectly on the mule's back. She must be standing on the level and not resting a hind foot. If the saddle is even slightly off center, the problem will get worse as you travel, and the cinch, the manties and the sling ropes loosen. A tight cinch, particularly, can disguise potential problems at this point. Lower the light side and raise the heavy side until the loads balance. Lowering is usually easier than raising, but with some loads you'll end up doing both.

Figure 81a-c. Knot used for pigtailing pack stock.

using the breakaway loop of quarter-inch manila or sissal that we told you to put on your saddles in chapter three. Figure 81 illustrates the knot we use to tie a lead rope to a pigtail. This is a self-tightening knot that remains easy to untie even when a horse has been hanging back on it all day. We like to tie our pack stock just long enough that they can get their heads down to get a drink or graze when they're stopped. Any longer than this and you'll have mules getting forefeet over their lead rope or trying to eat as they walk down the trail. A mule who's eating isn't watching where she's going. Eventually she'll go on the wrong side of a tree or hang up in the brush, and you'll be lucky if the only thing that breaks is the pigtail.

Tailing is the traditional method of linking animals in a pack string. We don't recommend that you use it though. Some horses and mules just won't put up with having another animal tied to their tail, and because, like pigtails, horse tails will break away with a hard pull, sooner or later you'll find yourself with a string of short-tailed horses. Sore-tailed too. The most used knot for tailing is illustrated in Figure 82. It's a venerable piece of packer's lore, but the only reason we're teaching it to you is because it can be useful for leading a string of lost animals back to camp. You can't pigtail unsaddled stock.

Trailing loose horses and mules, like tailing, used to be common practice. Before the turn of the century, commercial packers often used large strings to move freight long distances. For them, driving pack animals was a necessary expedient, made feasible by unfenced country and little or no competing traffic. In parts of Colorado, Wyoming, California and the Canadian Rockies, some packers still trail stock, but trailing is a technique whose time has

c.

passed. Loose animals cause too many
problems: they eat; they cut switch backs
and go banging around in the brush; they
create problems for other packers you meet
on the trail; they make it hard to keep an eye
on your loads. Ultimately loose stock will
do more damage to the country and your
gear. Control your animals.

The first animal in a string should be one
who leads easily and who won't kick at a
horse or mule behind. Many packers put
their fastest mule at the head of the string. If
you do this, you'll not only break a lot of
pigtails, but you'll teach your slower
animals that they can break loose whenever
they're tired of being pulled. We suggest
you select a steady, slower animal to go
first, one with a walking pace that the entire
string will find comfortable and who won't
be always running up on your saddle horse
or trying to pass him.

Put your quicker, more agile animals
toward the end of the string where their
greater athletic ability will help them
negotiate obstacles. Progressively taller
animals toward the end of a string make it
easier for you to see how the loads back
there are riding. A problem animal, like a
puller who knows how to break pigtails or a
round-backed mule who's saddle often
slips, should go second. There you can keep
an eye on him and let him know from time
to time that his behavior is being
scrutinized. If he does break a pigtail, he's
less likely to head over the nearest ridge if
he's dragging the whole string, and if a
saddle slips on a narrow trail, you won't
have to squeeze past the whole string to
adjust it.

a.

Figure 82a-c. Knot used for tailing
pack stock. This is something you may
never have to do, but it's a good thing
to know.

Keep your strings short, and you'll enjoy
life more. Leading two or three pack
animals isn't difficult. Leading six to ten,
even though some packers do it routinely, is
a real headache. Short strings of five or less
are faster, and in a large party with many
animals, several short strings will give
more people a hand in moving the camp.

116

a. *b.*

Figure 83a-b. Mount with the lead rope in your left hand to avoid being caught around the waist half-way into the saddle.

When all the horses and mules are loaded, take a last look around to be sure you haven't left anything. Put your wallet in your saddle bags so the cantle doesn't work it out of your hip pocket, and you're ready to go.

Your string is more likely to stand quietly while you mount and get organized if you start with your saddle horse facing the pack string. You'll also find it easier to mount when you're leading a string if you hold the lead rope on your left side and in your rein hand. That way you won't find yourself stopped half-way into the saddle by a lead rope around your waist. Once you're on, you can switch the lead rope to your right hand if that's more comfortable. Pulling a string can get tiring, and you'll probably change hands from time to time anyway.

Resist the suicidal urge to tie the pack string to your saddle horn. If a pack animal slips off a trail or shies suddenly, he can pull your saddle horse over, jerk you out of the saddle or trap you in it. Pigtails will break but nylon lead rope won't. Neither will saddle horns. We don't think you should even dally, since even a single full turn can jam on itself. If a mule is hanging back, you can relieve the strain on your arm

by taking a half turn around the horn (Figure 84). You'll be amazed how easy it is to pull a reluctant pack animal with that little bit of mechanical advantage. With a half turn around the horn and a string that's keeping up, you can have a free hand for a sandwich or a map simply by tucking the end of the lead rope under your knee. If you can't keep a horse or mule following with half a dally, loop the lead rope over her nose as described in chapter two. We guarantee that this will take the strain off your arm and your saddle horse who otherwise has to pull the mule along.

*Figure 84.
A safe dally
for leading stock.
This won't jam
and can be released
simply by moving
your knee.*

*Figure 85.
The more difficult
the terrain, the more
time you must spend
looking back at your
string. Even on easy
trails, a pack string
demands considerable
attention.*
Harley Hettick

Don't be shy about talking to your animals. If you move out without waking up the mules dozing at the end of the string, you'll find yourself breaking pigtails. Call out their names as you start your saddle horse. Many horsemen think that names for horses and mules are foolishness, and they get along without them by referring to the big mare, the fat gelding or the speckled mule. Horses and mules do learn their names, and though they won't respond to them the way a dog will, yelling at Stumblefoot will make him quit watching Pathfinder's tail before he trips over that log in the trail. A rider following a string should also talk to the animals to keep them moving and help them past obstacles.

Leading stock means that you're going to have to give up about half your scenery-watching time and devote it to looking back at the string. Even an experienced string demands a lot of attention. On a level trail with no bends or obstacles, you can get away with a quick backward glance every hundred feet or so. As the terrain gets more difficult, more and more of your time must be devoted to watching pack stock. Sighting between each mule's ears, you should see the D-rings or cross bucks of the pack saddles centered on every back. If a saddle is listing, you'll have to stop and raise or lower loads to get better balance.

Occasionally you'll find that you've

*Figure 86.
Large parties
will travel faster
and with fewer
problems if the
pack stock is broken
up into several
short strings.*
Harley Hettick

moved both packs as much as you can, and they still won't balance. You could take them off, open them up and move something from the heavy side to the light side. But this is a bother and extremely time consuming. The quick and dirty solution is to wedge a rock in the manty ropes of the light load. This isn't very elegant — in fact it's considered bad form — but in practice everyone does it because it works. If you've made an honest effort to balance your loads and failed, don't be proud.

Properly mantied loads shouldn't come apart, but we humans are fallible and occasionally our imperfect works fail. When you spot a problem, stop, tie up your horse and the string, and correct it immediately, or at any rate before the saddle goes under the pack animal or gear begins trickling out along the trail. If you're caught in the open with nothing to tie up to, use the nose-to-nose trick mentioned earlier. Turn your saddle horse so he faces the lead mule in the pack string, tie an overhand loop in the lead rope and drape it over the saddle horn. For this to work, your horse and that lead mule have to get along. If there's any chance your horse is going to lead the string down the trail the moment you turn your back, hobble him.

Little problems like unbalanced loads and loose girths can be handled quickly with the pack animal in place in the string. But for major adjustments where you're going to be removing and possibly remantying loads, its a good idea to take the animal involved out of the string. And unless the pack animal has excellent withers or you know for a fact that he doesn't mind a manty under his belly, remove both loads or have a helper support the remaining manty whenever you have one off.

You'll make the best time — and over the long run your stock will lead better — by maintaining a steady pace. If all loads stayed together and in place, if all trails were flat and straight without streams or down timber (maybe in Kansas?), you might stand a fighting chance of realizing this even-paced ideal. Streams, deadfall, mud, hills, and switchbacks conspire to keep you aware of where you are and what you're doing — leading horses and mules along winding mountain trails.

When you're on the move, the most important thing you can do is remember the plight of the last animals in the string. Time and again we've seen packers cross a stream, ride up the far bank and put their horse back into high gear while the last pack animals are still picking their way across the rocky bottom. Pack stock needs as much time or more to get over a log or around a sharp bend as you allowed your saddle horse.

Short dips in the trail are not obviously obstacles, but they can pose problems for your pack stock unless you recognize them as such. Your horse and all trailing animals will sit back as they start down. You've got to hold your horse back until the last pack animal is down on the level.

River crossings, particularly in the early season, can be treacherous and demand special skills. Even small streams can cause

Figure 87.
Crossing deadfall.
Hold your saddle horse
back and watch the
string until the last
animal is over. The
same principle applies
to any obstacle.
Harley Hettick

problems when the water is roiling and muddy. Look all crossings over carefully. If there's any doubt about a string's ability to cross easily, a single rider on an experienced, surefooted horse should cross first to check depth, bottom characteristics and current strength. There's a huge difference in footing between a sandy or gravelly bottom and a bottom of large, mossy boulders. Similarly, fast water, deeper than a horse's belly, exerts its force against a much wider surface than water swirling around a horse's thin legs.

On all crossings, even of smaller streams, strings should be angled into the current. This gives the stock better balance against the force of the current (just like loading diagonally in a large trailer) and counteracts a natural tendency to move downstream. Even when wading shallow water, a pack string will drift. The last mule will always end up further downstream than the mule ahead.

In a bad crossing, one where there's a chance of a mule or horse going down or having to swim, loads should be retied with a barrel hitch. A tight, properly tied manty will keep out water for a long time and provides some additional buoyancy. Barrel-hitched loads, tied down against the

horse or mule act like pontoons. Basket-hitched loads, in contrast, will float up and away from a swimming animal. Panyards used without a diamond hitched pack cover should also be tied down.

Bad crossings are one time that driving loose pack horses can be a good idea. Each horse or mule picks his own way, and if one goes down or slips, he won't start a chain reaction.

Occasionally an even more drastic technique, skylining, is called for. Skylining involves stretching a rope across the stream or river two to three feet above the water. Each pack animal's lead rope is then tied with a bowline to this rope, and the animal is pulled across with a third rope tied into the bowline. Skylining keeps each animal pointed upstream. Where the water isn't quite deep enough to make him swim, it provides a fifth point of balance. Obviously at least one rider has to be able to cross to set up a skyline, so the technique isn't for impossible crossings. Instead it has its greatest application at extremely narrow fords — in a steep gorge for example — where the tendency of pack animals to drift downstream as they cross may bring them to shore below the only point where the banks allow them to get out.

120

*Figure 88a-b.
Crossing rivers is unavoidable in roadless country and can be dangerous. It's always wise to cross downstream from potentially dangerous snags.*

a.

Everyone with a TV has seen the Marlboro man or one of his ilk ride into the Pecos sitting tall in the saddle while his horse swims calmly across. That might sell cigarettes or movie tickets, but swimming horses isn't something you should do for fun as an episode recorded by fur trapper Osborne Russell in 1835 shows dramatically.

> ...we were obliged to cross Lewis Fork [of the Snake River in Idaho] which is about 300 yds wide and might be forded at a low stage of water, but at present was almost overflowing its banks and running at the rate of about 6 mls per hour. We commenced making a boat by sewing two raw Bulls hides together.... Our boat being completed we commenced crossing our equippage and while 5 of us were employed at this a young man by the name of Abram Patterson attempted to cross on horse back in spite of all the advice and entreaty of those present his wild and rash temper got the better of his reason and after a desperate struggle to reach the opposite bank he abandoned his horse, made a few springs and sunk to rise no more — he was a native of Penna. about 23 years of age. We succeeded in crossing our baggage and encamped at the East side for the night.

> Osborne Russell, Aubrey L. Haines, ed.
> *Journal of a Trapper*
> University of Nebraska Press
> Lincoln, 1965

b.

If you have to swim your horse across a river — and we mean have to — you should plan on getting wet. By staying in the saddle, you're only weighting your horse down and making him work harder. You're also raising his center of gravity, and a round horse in moving water isn't too stable to begin with. Like a canoe, he has a tendency to be rolled over by the water flowing under and against him.

If you suspect your horse may have to swim, tie a knot in your reins. Loose, split reins dragging in the water may tangle on a horse's legs or yours. Tie the reins short enough that he can't get a leg through them. Then ride into the water until it gets deep. Before your horse starts to swim, slip out of the saddle on the downstream side and float, holding onto the saddle horn. In this position, even if the horse doesn't have to swim, your body will act as an outrigger, counteracting his tendency to roll.

Where there is a chance of the horse being washed against a boulder or a snag, your safest position is behind the horse. In this case, slide off the back and hold onto the tail. Don't worry about getting kicked. You'll be towed along well behind your swimming horse's feet.

Children, poor swimmers, inexperienced riders or any combination of these are particularly vulnerable on river crossings. Smaller horses and ponies, though often more surefooted, are more easily upset in deep, flowing water because they are shorter and lighter. Also, a child not only lacks an appreciation for the dangers of a crossing, but may not be a forceful enough rider to help or correct a horse that slips or panics. Your best alternative, if your saddle horse can be ridden double, is to take the child across behind you and lead the child's horse. On safer crossings, the child can stay on his own horse, but you should lead him. One friend of our routinely carries life jackets for his young daughters when he takes them packing. Life jackets weigh little

and are a good idea for any weak rider or poor swimmer who might be pitched off if a horse slips. Even a strong swimmer can't help himself if he's unconscious.

Crossing rivers is a part of the wilderness experience. Some risk adds piquance to the experience, and something would be lost if every stream were bridged, every ford sandy-bottomed and ankle deep. Still, swimming and skylining horses are techniques for extreme situations, and while you should know how to deal with such conditions, we don't suggest you seek them out.

Beyond every river is a hill. And if crossing rivers is part of wilderness riding, so is crossing passes. Nearly everyone realizes his string needs rest stops during a long climb, and there's no special trick to timing such rests. When your saddle horse is breathing hard and has worked up a good sweat, it's time to stop. Less appreciated is the fact that a string should be rested with about the same frequency on long downhill stretches. Holding back with a 200-pound load is hard work for a mule and though the fatigue is less obvious, the need for rest is no less real.

Frequent, short rest stops are better than a few long stops. The longer your animals stand, the greater the chance that some joker in the string will wander off the trail in search of a snack or will pick a fight with the mule in front of him. If the whole string seems to be wandering around looking for trouble, the old loafers aren't as tired as you thought, and you should get them moving. Stopping in narrow places, hemmed in by

dense brush or steep slopes also minimizes the ways a mule or horse can get in trouble.

Leading a string isn't particularly hard, but it takes practice and experience. The only way to get either is to go out and do it. Smoke likes to compare leading a pack string to driving a train. That's a good anology in a mechanical sense, but pulling mules is also a bit like taking a kindergarten class on a field trip. When they're fresh, well fed and rested, horses and mules have a five-year-old's capacity for daydreaming and for non-malicious mischief.

So far we've talked only about the mechanics of traveling with pack stock, but there's a human side to this primitive way of travel, an aspect that's easily overlooked in an age when most travel is in cars that hurtle us down the highway, sealed off from other travelers by molded glass and steel. We go to the hills, in part at least, to get away from people, knowing, of course, that other's are doing the same thing, and we'll almost certainly fail any quest for total solitude. So in another sense we should go

to the hills looking for people, knowing that those few we meet can and should be treated in a more human, personal way than is customary when people are everywhere.

Encounters between pack strings and other pack strings or hikers are, to some extent, governed by custom. These customs are a little like traffic laws, but with important differences: they aren't laws, and writing them here is a far cry from engraving them on stone tablets. Also, there's no clear hierarchy among these rules, and at times they conflict. When they do, there's no recourse to a higher authority. Who wants traffic cops in the Wind Rivers or the high Sierra? When you meet another packer on a narrow trail, which of you is entitled to the right-of-way is less important than how you work things out between yourselves. Our rules are only guidelines and life is too short and too sweet to waste it arguing about who should turn around. Leave your alienation and your temper in your car.

Uphill strings have the right-of-way in

123

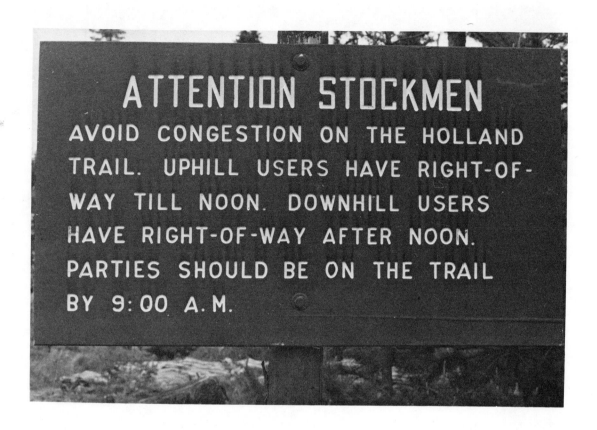

ATTENTION STOCKMEN
AVOID CONGESTION ON THE HOLLAND
TRAIL. UPHILL USERS HAVE RIGHT-OF-
WAY TILL NOON. DOWNHILL USERS
HAVE RIGHT-OF-WAY AFTER NOON.
PARTIES SHOULD BE ON THE TRAIL
BY 9:00 A.M.

the morning, downhill strings have it in the afternoon. Think about this for a moment, and you'll see that it makes sense. Trailheads and campsites tend to be at lower elevations, so for a pack string that gets on the trail before the crack of noon, the rule mirrors the natural order of things.

When two strings meet on the level, the shorter string turns or gets off the trail. If both are the same length, the downhill string turns. Same length on the dead level? Well, you can flip a coin, or arm wrestle or be a nice guy and volunteer. You weren't in a hurry anyway.

Turning on a narrow trail can be tricky. The easiest way is to turn each mule and horse in place. First tie your saddle horse to the mule who led the string. Work backward until the last mule becomes the lead mule. On foot, lead the string back to a place where the other string can pass, and you can regroup. On steep sidehills try to work on the downhill side of your animals. This may be hard on your vertigo, but your stock will be calmer. As we mentioned

earlier, horses were prey animals for hundreds of thousands of years, and they retain a prey species's nervousness about other animals, like yourself, above them.

One of the most common violations of backcountry courtesy is visiting on horseback in someone else's camp. Folks who would scream if you walked into their living room with manure on your boots, think nothing of riding right into camp to visit. Don't do this. If you want to stop and chew the fat, tie up your string well away from camp, ideally in a rocky area or a lodgepole thicket where no one is going to want to camp later. If someone rides into your camp, ask him to get his horse out of your living room. He's being rude, not you.

In most areas, hikers outnumber packers and always will. There's a potential conflict between the two styles of travel, and though the reasons for this are many and complex, there's no point in aggravating the situation. Hikers and packers are fundamentally in search of the same values. Although for generations horse travel has been the predominant mode of travel in the mountain west, in this case, first in time is not first in right. An arrogant, we-were-here-first attitude will get horsemen nowhere. The Indians were here first and look at what happened to them.

As with encounters between two pack strings there are established conventions governing encounters between pack strings and walkers. Problems arise because packers are more likely to be familiar with these conventions — which generally give the less maneuverable pack string the right-of-way — than are backpackers. Also, many backpackers lack experience around stock and don't know what to expect from passing stock or how to behave to avoid spooking them. Successfully getting your horses and mules past hikers on the trail depends on you. You are going to have to suggest appropriate behavior, and do this without seeming arrogant or peremptory.

Hikers should be asked to step off the trail on the downhill side and stand quietly. You might want to explain that a backpack

changes a human's shape and that your animals may shy. Asking people to stand off the trail is as much for their benefit and safety as yours.

Most pack strings travel faster than a walking person, and while it may not seem possible to you when you are at the head of a clomping, squeaking train of animals and gear, you can sneak up behind hikers and scare the daylights out of them. Not only is this inconsiderate, it can be hazardous. In bear country, and particularly in grizzly country, many hikers carry bear-bells, and we've noticed a disturbing tendency for more and more hikers to carry a pistol on their hip. You don't want a startled hiker spinning around and frantically ringing a bell in your horse's face, and you certainly don't want holes shot in your new Stetson. Call out a warning "howdy" as you come up behind hikers.

Perhaps the greatest rudeness you can direct at hikers is stopping to visit without dismounting. This is an unconscious thing for most riders — we stop to chat about the

Figure 90.
Two strings meeting.
The string in the foreground
has moved off the trail
to let the other string
pass. In this case, the
string that moved out of
the way could do so
more easily than the other.
Harley Hettick

125

Harley Hettick

fishing or trail conditions and stay in the saddle — but it conveys overtones of differences in status: the plantation owner inspecting his field hands, the squire visiting his crofters. You may not feel this from nine feet in the air, but the walker who has to talk up to you will be uncomfortable. Swinging off is easy enough, and your knees will appreciate the chance to straighten for a while.

Finally you can minimize conflicts between packers and hikers by being a little self-serving at the same time you're being neighborly and helpful. If, for example, a group of hikers asks about good campsites, don't send them to the big meadows where you camped last night. Instead suggest the small glade by the river where you crossed a few miles back or the alpine lake you've always wanted to fish but couldn't because there was no feed for your stock. By doing this you lessen the chances that some other packer will come along behind you and find the only grass for ten miles in either

direction taken up by four hikers, grazing 30 square feet of nylon tents.

Finally, we urge you to make an effort to cooperate with rangers, management agencies like the Forest Service, and land owners. Except in National Parks, private packers are subject to little or no regulation. If a backcountry ranger suggests you avoid a campsite because it's being overgrazed or that you stay out of a valley because of crowding or fire danger, do it, even if it means changing your plans. The alternative to voluntary cooperation will be a system of permits and use allocation similar to the regulations already imposed in most national parks and on commercial outfitters on Forest Service lands.

Whomever you meet in the backcountry, etiquette distills to a single, simple rule: Be courteous. Courtesy costs nothing, and in extending it as a matter of course to fellow wanderers, we believe you'll reap more of the elusive rewards that make time spent in wild, empty country so alluring.

Figure 91.
A camp on
Albino Creek,
Bob Marshall
Wilderness.

chapter eight
Camps

As I write this, I am in a good camp. Down the meadow and downstream from our camp there is more than enough grass for our seven head of stock — two mules and five horses. Ten yards below the cook tent, where the mules aren't likely to find it, a spring rises cold and pure from a small basin, before trickling off to join the main creek. Our tents shelter against the forest at the west end of the meadow and are close to the return trail without straddling it.

The stock is grazing intently now on the rich bunch grasses near the creek. Once their bellies are full they may grow restless, and should one take a notion to head for the truck, eight miles away, we are in a perfect position to see them and head them off. A simple pole drift fence, fifty yards up the trail, will bring any such homing urges to a sudden if temporary halt, and gives us a welcome margin of security.

The fence is technically a violation of the wilderness prohibition on permanent structures, but it was here, so we used it. Similarly, a hitch rail and poles which we used to erect our cook fly add amenity. But they do not make this a good camp, and, in fact, they detract slightly from the wilderness ambience.

The most important features are ample grass and conveniently located water for the stock. Next in importance are sheltered, well-drained tent sites, abundant firewood and scenery. For the horse packer, the first rule of campsite selection is "think of your stock," and a corollary is that your site should permit you to hold and care for your animals without damaging the country. Only when you can satisfy these requirements can you begin to factor in your comfort, both physical and esthetic. Your first obligation is to your animals. The integrity of the wilderness runs a close second, and your personal comfort a rather distant third.

The three aren't nearly as distinct as this makes them sound. For instance, a great deal of my personal satisfaction derives from watching my horses grazing contentedly, and knowing that I am doing everything possible to keep the impact of my camp at a minimum. When we leave, this place will hardly be different than when we came.

Figure 92. The most important features of a packer's camp site are ample grass and water for the stock.

We, by the way, does not this time include Smoke. He is camped some 30 miles to the northeast, having disappeared into his "living room," as he refers to the Bob Marshall Wilderness, shortly after we planned this chapter in late June. Between that time and September 1, he will leave the mountains only one day. He, too, is in a good camp, a place called Murphy Flat. Interestingly, my camp would not be a good one for Smoke. With him are ten guests, and 21 head of saddle and pack stock. This relatively small meadow simply couldn't hold that many animals without experiencing considerable range damage.

A few weeks ago I rode into the Bob Marshall to meet Smoke. On the way I passed a large camp, located rather perplexingly in an open grove of lodgepole pine. The view from the campsite was uninspiring at best, and the pasture was almost nonexistent. It was mid-afternoon, so the camp had not been there long. Hungry horses and mules — about twenty in all — were ranging restlessly through the trees, and two riders were in the saddle, working hard to keep the stock from heading out for greener pastures. They weren't going to get much sleep; if they did, they would be up early hunting horses.

There is no reason, barring atrocious weather, that you can't have most of the elements of a good camp — good for you, your animals and the country — nearly every time you stop. This takes planning, organization, and the self-discipline to recognize that there are places, however beautiful, where simply because you are traveling with stock, you cannot or should not camp. Among these are high alpine areas, mossy-shored lakes, small wooded glades, and, of course, occupied sites.

When traveling in country you know, you should have a campsite in mind as well as a backup in case your first choice is occupied. Never camp near another party. Courtesy demands that you respect others' desire for solitude. You must also be organized enough that you allow yourself ample time to get to your camp. When planning ahead, remember that you often have better feed, particularly in late summer or fall, by going a mile or two off main routes to less-used campsites. Even if your stock might scrape by on heavily grazed pasture, you should be considerate of the range. Smoke tries never to repeat a campsite twice in the same summer.

Traveling in new country adds considerably to the uncertainty of finding a

Figure 93. The Bob Marshall Wilderness, looking west down White River toward the South Fork of the Flathead and the Swan Range.

good place to camp. Not only do you not know where the best campsites are, your natural exploratory urges, the ones that prompted you into a new area in the first place, will incline you to pass up a satisfactory campsite by making you wonder if there isn't something just a little better further down the trail.

One solution is the leave-nothing-to-chance approach where you make extensive inquiries in advance and plan a detailed itinerary based on the advice of other packers, rangers or guidebooks. In some highly controlled settings, such as national parks, this is your only alternative. The National Park Service requires backcountry camp/fire permits. Other agencies prefer that you obtain these even though they are optional.

The other possible approach is to go in cold with only a map and the general knowledge that you can find feed for your stock. No matter how strong your urge to explore, you have an obligation to your stock to make inquiries in advance about the availability of feed. In some mountain ranges, there is little or no pasture.

If you yield to the temptation to follow your nose, you should set some ground rules for yourself so you aren't forced by darkness to camp in the middle of the trail or in wooded sites without feed. Don't plan on covering a lot of miles each day. Instead, decide you will take the first acceptable campsite you find after a set time — say two or three in the afternoon. If you want the thrill of exploring unknown country, you're going to have to live with the chance that you're stopping short of a better camp around the next ridge.

Regardless of which approach you choose, you should check with the nearest Forest Service ranger district when entering any national forest. By giving the Forest Service even a general idea of your plans, you add considerably to your safety, particularly during the late-summer fire season.

Before you ride into a potential campsite, stop with your animals on the periphery and look it over. Decide whether it's what you want, and plan the camp layout. While you sit and think, your pack stock will have a few minutes to relieve themselves outside camp rather than in the middle of your kitchen while you're unloading.

First decide if there's enough feed for your stock for the number of days you plan to stay. Judging the amount of available feed is largely a matter of experience, but you also have to know not only what horses will eat, but also what types of grasses and

Figure 94. Although the feed along lakes and in marshy areas appears to be lush, it is rarely as nutrious as grass on drier sites.

forbs will do them some good. A carpet of green doesn't guarantee good grazing, and can be deceiving. In our country, beargrass stays green throughout the year and covers large expanses of open meadow. But beargrass is worthless as feed except as a belly filler when nothing else is available. Horses and mules on their first trip into the hills quickly learn that despite its apparent succulence, beargrass isn't worth the energy required to reach down and nip it off. Similarly the lush green sedges and rushes of low swampy areas may look good to you, but they won't keep your stock going strong. Sedges look like grass but have angular rather than round stems — some sedges do make good feed, particularly in alpine areas. The native western grasses — fescues, wheatgrasses, bluegrasses — make the best feed and remain highly nutritious even when cured. Timothy, though not a native, also makes excellent pasture. It has been introduced in most back country areas in hay and manure and now grows extensively around good campsites.

While you're thinking about range for your stock, give some thought to wildlife. Livestock grazing can be detrimental to deer and elk if it removes feed they would otherwise use in winter. You should avoid open south-facing slopes of grass and shrubs at low elevations. In late summer, the grass on north and east slopes will be better, and yet worthless to wildlife in winter.

If the grass will hold your stock, you can begin laying out camp. Camp well off the trail, but ideally between your stock and the trail you arrived on. Horse's who go in for after-hours travel most often head back towards the last camp or the trailhead. Tent sites should be on level, but slightly elevated ground so there is good drainage. Never ditch — if you find you have to, you chose a poor tent site. Even a poor tent won't need a ditch if it's on a slight hump, and ditching won't help the best tent if its in a hole. Not only are ditches useless, they are eyesores that can't be eradicated when you leave. They become permanent scars on the landscape; they encourage erosion; and they subtly pressure others to pitch their tents in the same places and with the same orientation if only to avoid lying across your ditches. Continually reused tent sites become patches of bare ground, packed too hard to support grass. Each time it rains they become muddy and erode.

Your tents should also be well away from dead trees and the base of cliffs, anywhere something might fall and indefinitely prolong someone's sleep. Make a practice of

Figure 95. Hay and manure have planted timothy throughout the backcountry.

taking off your hat and looking up before you settle on a tent site. A wide brim screens out the view above six feet, and snags are easily overlooked.

It's nice, but not essential, to locate your kitchen area near water and firewood. But shade, shelter from the wind, and a safe place for a stove or fire are equally important. A hundred yards isn't too far to carry water, and you can always use a pack horse to haul firewood. Resist the urge to plant your camp right on the edge of a lake or stream. Both the Forest Service and the National Park Service recommend that camps be a minimum of 100 feet from water. You won't sacrifice much by honoring this suggestion, and a walk for water in the morning or evening can be a pleasant respite from the inevitable bustle around the kitchen.

You should also try to exert some control over where your stock waters. Pick a spot downstream from where you get water and where the bank can stand constant coming and going. A ford is good. So are low gravel banks. You can encourage all your stock to water in this place by leading one or two animals there shortly after coming into camp. Pack animals tend to water in a group; the others will follow those who first decide they are thirsty. Once they use a place, they will come back to it again and again.

A final decision before riding into camp is the location of your picket area. This should be well way from trails and your living area, in a place where no one is likely to want to camp. Rocky areas and lodgepole thickets are good.

When you finally ride into camp, go directly to this picket area, tie the saddle horses and loosen their cinches. Then lead the pack stock to the center of camp and unload quickly. If the stock is tired and you

have enough hands, one person can lead the string between two others, who drop and pile loads. If you're short-handed or have a long string, you'll find it easier to bring pack animals into camp one or two at a time to be unloaded. As soon as the loads are off, take them back to the picket area, tie them short, and leave them to cool off with loosened cinches. How long they should stand depends on how hot the day and the horses are.

Smoke likes to set up sleeping tents and

Figure 96. "First things first."

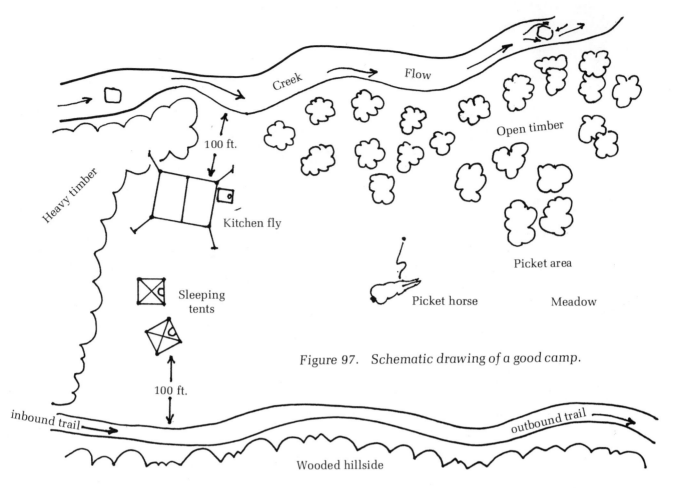

latrines first since the comfort of his guests is the paramount consideration. They can then be busy organizing their personal gear, washing or fishing while Smoke organizes the kitchen. For private parties, the order is probably best reversed. I like to get the cook tent up and the gear under it, particularly if the weather is bad. Then fire up the stove and put the coffee on. First things first!

One of the big advantages of a cook stove is that you don't have to alter the stove site. Stove legs transmit very little heat, and if you toss a few shovels-full of dirt or sand in the bottom of the stove, almost no heat radiates downward. There's no need to disturb the sod. A few flat rocks under the stove door make an adequate hearth. If conditions are very dry, you should soak this area with a bucket of water. Otherwise the only precautions you need take are to clear needles and dead branches from the hearth area and make sure that the stove pipe isn't aimed into the crown of a tree.

The only safe surface for an open fire is bare, mineral soil. All sod on your fire site should be removed over an area at least one foot larger in diameter than your fire will be. Don't stack the sod around the edge of the fire ring. Put it off to one side and you can replace it when you leave. Under very dry conditions, soak the perifery of the fire ring. If you need rocks to support a grill, use as few as possible. Your fire will burn better if it's not completely enclosed, and you will be minimizing your contribution to black-rock blight. There are far too many blackened fire sites dotting the mountains. You should use existing fire rings rather than making new ones. When you leave camp, obliterate even these. Fire rings are easily spaded up and buried.

Wood chips from cutting and splitting firewood also blight a campsite. Chips, like orange peels, stay around a long time. The solution is to cut and split wood where you find it rather than in camp. This means a little extra work, but not much. When you gather wood, take a manty with you and pile the cut, split stove lengths on it. Then gather the corners together and carry the bundle back to camp.

The best firewood is standing dead

timber. Wood that's been on the ground even a single winter won't burn as hot. An ethical problem arises because numerous small mammals and birds depend on standing snags for nesting cavities. Biologists are finding that many of these species have declined due to a shortage of suitable housing. You can minimize your impact if you don't cut snags with broken tops or a diameter greater than five inches. Your best alternative is dead and down timber with the bark still on but beginning to separate from the bole. In this country, down conifers without bark are usually punky, but that's not true everywhere.

There are endless arguments about what makes the best firewood. These hinge on heat efficiency, but for camp situations they miss the point. Take whatever is available. Often that's lodgepole. As conifers go, lodgepole burns cleanly and with good heat. It generally is available in convenient diameters — under 5 inches — and it splits easily.

The one remaining feature of your camp is toilet facilities. Anything we advocate on this score is likely to draw disagreement from someone. Since Smoke is the sole responsible party on his trips, he has to control sanitation. In every camp, his wranglers dig latrines — his and hers — shielded by tents. Both the Forest Service and the National Park Service, however, advocate a one-time latrine: a small hole, one shovel full, in the top four to six inches of soil. This includes the biologically active layer of the soil, and the thinking is that the earth is better able to handle waste disposal when the problem is spread out rather than concentrated.

How to reconcile these conflicting situations? It seems to us that both methods have their place and neither is best or even acceptable 100 per cent of the time. The officially endorsed, one-time-hole method is best suited to small groups of at least moderately experienced wilderness users and to short stays in moderate to low-use areas. Large groups, long stays, heavily used camp sites and inexperienced campers all argue for the more controlled central facility. In this case, the camp equipment should include a coffee can of lime. Evaluate your own situation, and do what seems best. Make sure that everyone in your party understands how sanitation will be practiced. With the one-time-hole method, make sure that everyone understands what type of area they should wander off to when they pick up the shovel and the toilet paper: downwind, well away from camp, trails, water and potential campsites. The all-purpose lodgepole thicket is good again.

Other sanitation problems you must deal with are garbage, waste water and washing (clothes, dishes and bodies). Burnable garbage can and should be burned. That includes paper, peelings and left-over food. Aluminum foil doesn't burn. Other garbage, bottles and cans, should be stored in a heavy plastic garbage bag and packed out. Before consigning them to the garbage sack, cans should be washed or burned out. The idea is to avoid packing garbage that smells like garbage. Besides tainting the

Figure 98a-b.
Use soap
or detergent
to wash pots
and dishes,
but don't use
either in lakes
or streams.

a.

rest of your outfit, the smell of garbage attracts bears. Save space by flattening cans.

Most bear problems occur in or near national parks where bears are not hunted and cease to fear humans. They learn they can raid camps with impunity. In parts of Yosemite, the bear population is far greater than the natural food supply can support and reflects the bears' incredible adeptness at stealing campers' food. The only defense is to hang food in trees, and in national parks with bear problems, like Yosemite, Yellowstone and Glacier, it is required that you do so. Hanging food so bears can't get it is difficult, and the more food you have, the harder the job will be. If you pack in the national parks, you will find it easier to forgo fresh food in favor of lighter, more odor-free freeze-dried food.

The only method of hanging food that we have found to be consistently effective is suspend it at least ten feet off the ground between two trees that are at least 15 feet apart. This takes a lot of rope, and unless the trees are easily climbed or have branches in just the right places it takes a lot of time and patience as well. Where bears have learned to steal food, hanging it in a single tree, no matter how high or how far out from the trunk, probably won't do the job.

Having bears around is not the same thing as having bear problems. In most national forests where bears are hunted and camp-raiding bears are often harassed, bears are wary of people. They will rarely come into a camp in search of food. Despite the fact that the Bob Marshall Wilderness has both black and grizzly bears, nearly everyone who packs there simply leaves food boxes on the ground under the kitchen fly. Hanging the total weight of food in most packer's camps is simply out of the question.

In most places, the greatest risk to your camp occurs when camp is left untended. When leaving camp, you should take special pains to be sure that food boxes are closed up tightly, that stoves, tables and kitchen utensils are clean, and that there is no garbage or food lying around. A final precaution — one that may do more for your peace of mind than it does to deter bears — is to liberally sprinkle black pepper around the kitchen area. We do this when we are away from hunting camp overnight or longer. Other people rub their tents with

b.

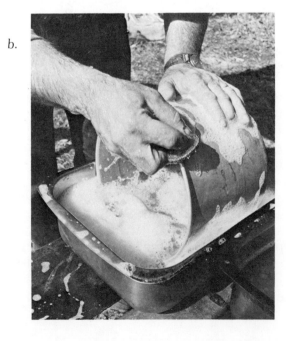

onion or garlic. We'd rather be visited by bears. Do these things work? It's hard to be sure. Obviously we think that pepper has some deterrent value. It's an easy thing to do, but it's not a substitute for a clean camp.

Don't wash anything in streams or lakes using soap or detergent. Soap is soap no matter how biodegradable it's supposed to be. Anything includes yourself. Your kitchen should include a pair of basins, one for washing, the other for rinsing. These can do multiple duty for clothes washing, shaving and baths.

Don't cut corners washing dishes. Dishes should be washed in warm water with soap or detergent. Detergent is better at cutting grease and has less disastrous consequences for your gastrointestinal tract than soap if you fail to rinse thoroughly. Use a low-phosphate brand. Rinse dishes in hot — preferably boiling — water. Lots of campers say they get away with a less strict dish washing regimen, but don't be beguiled by such talk. No one likes to wash dishes, but the little extra effort required to do it right is well worth it. Your trip won't be much fun if you have to run off into the bushes every half hour.

Scatter dishwater on the ground well away from any streams or lakes. A sump for dishwater is an unnecessary hole.

Bathing is where most people's good intentions face a severe test and often fail. Sooner or later — sooner if the days are hot and the trails dusty — your sense of dirtiness will become overwhelming and a soapless swim won't do the job. You rationalize: "The little bit of soap I'm going to get in that river won't hurt anything, and besides, if I don't take a real bath soon, I'm going to rot." So you hide a bar of soap in your towel and sneak off to make a ring around the river, leaving your guilty conscience in camp.

Before you succumb, we offer this alternative. Heat a basin of water and carry it with you to the creek. Leave it, your soap, your wash-cloth and towel on the bank, well back from the water. Then get wet. In the northern Rockies, unless you're extremely well insulated, a swim lasts about five seconds. Get out, go to the basin of hot water, and soap up. Wash everything you plan to wash. Then dump the water over your head. You're still soapy so fill the basin with water from the creek. Move back and finish rinsing. When you're soap free you can go back to the stream for a final dip. I find that even after the cold rinse my skin is still warm enough from the hot water that the river feels much warmer the second time.

This prohibition on using soap in fresh water is only one of several you must observe in order to leave your camp as unaltered as possible. At the risk of seeming unduly negative, we offer a list of don'ts: Don't build permanent structures. Don't pound nails in trees. Don't cut live trees. Don't dig unnecessary holes. And don't alter stream beds by building dams to hold beer, fish or perishables.

Streams are dynamic living things and if you start mucking around with the bottom, you risk changing the character of the stream and the surrounding bottom lands.

Refrigerator holes dug near a stream are bad ideas for the same reason. When the water rises, the hole becomes part of the stream bed setting up new currents and eddies and encouraging erosion. You can have a more effective cooler by putting perishables in a wet gunny sack and hanging it in a shady place where it will catch the breeze. Evaporative cooling will keep your beer surprisingly cool.

A certain amount of damage is inevitable, but you can minimize this by undertaking some campsite rehabilitation as you break camp. Bury the ashes from your stove or fire, but make sure they are completely out — you should be able to handle them — before you cover them with dirt. Hot coals can start a fire in the duff or among roots that can smolder for weeks before bursting into flame on the surface. Obscure the place you bury ashes with brush and natural liter. If you removed sod for a fire site, replace it and water it with a few buckets of water. Also water heavily-worn places — the front of the stove, and the entrances to tents. Scatter any manure around the picket area or in camp. Give any pile you see a kick. Scattered, it will dry and decay more quickly and will nurture fewer flys. Fill in any holes that pawing horses may have dug and disguise the location as you did your ashes. Poles used to erect tarps or tents should have any nails removed, and the poles should be scattered. Finally, give the camp area a last check for trash.

Stock Management

By the time the cook tent and stove are up, the horses and mules should be ready to unsaddle. You can stack saddles on a log or rack them on a pole lashed between two trees, but either practice exposes them to damage by gnawing rodents. There is no foolproof system for protecting your tack, but Smoke's is as good as any. He spreads a manty on the ground and stacks saddles on it. Then he covers this pile with a plastic tarp and tucks it in under the manty. Remember to leave out saddlepads that you're going to sleep on. (see Figure 56a.

In private parties, everyone shares responsibility for watching the stock. Nonetheless, its a good idea to make one person wrangler, preferably an experienced horseman, to watch the stock closely for the first hour or two they are out. Horses and mules that have worked all day will have their heads down eating most of this time, but they will also roll. If one stiffens up or acts lame or colicky, you want to know about it right away. In a campsite new to the horses, there will also be a certain amount of exploring going on, and it can be helpful if, after an hour or two, when bellies start

Figure 100. A good nose bag.

filling up, someone has been watching which way the herd is drifting.

Horses and mules that are working every day need a lot of feed, at least 20 to 25 pounds of hay a day or an equivalent amount of grass, which, because it is wet, will weigh even more. Individual horses vary considerably in their feed requirements, but a good approximation is 2 percent of body weight in dry weight of feed a day. The same approximation holds for most large mammals, including humans. How long a horse has to graze to fill his belly and meet his nutritional requirements — the two aren't necessarily the same — depends primarily on the quality of the pasture. Where grass is thick and continuous and a horse can put his head down and eat on a straight line, six hours of feeding in a 24-hour period is probably a minimum. Where forage is sparse — a nip here, a mouthful there — he'll need considerably more time feeding.

If you have enough animals to pack it, some concentrated feed like oats or pellets every day is good insurance. We prefer pellets. They are weed free — you're not planting oats or anything else that doesn't belong in the back country — and their large size means that even if you feed them off the ground, little is wasted.

Nose bags are the best way to feed, but mean carrying additional equipment. Figure 100 shows the types Smoke uses. The extra strap around the neck helps the horse or mule keep the feed shaken down in the bag where he can reach it. Feeding off the ground isn't a good idea unless the stock is tied. Otherwise, dominant animals will get more than their share. There's also considerable waste when horses eat off the ground, and at the same time they ingest extraneous materials like dirt and rocks. Tying, however, means that you'd better stand and watch while they eat so no one gets a foot over a low rope.

A third, rather time consuming alternative, is to go from mule to horse with a pan of pellets. The theory is that they all have about the same mouth capacity and when its full, they have to stop gobbling up feed momentarily to chew and swallow. By going from animal to animal, giving each one mouthful at a time, you can evenly distribute a ration of feed with very little waste. Practice doesn't always follow theory, however, and some animals learn to shovel away the feed without a halt. You have to keep an eye on these chiselers. Nose bags are easier. Save your pennies and buy a few.

If you're feeding pellets, salt isn't necessary, but it will help you hold stock in a camp where you are staying for a few days. You should put salt where trampling won't cause too much damage, like a gravel pile or even the middle of the trail if traffic is light. Salt left lying on the ground in wet weather or for a long period of time, as it often is in a hunting camp, will leach into the ground creating an artificial lick that will attract wildlife. Avoid this. Deer that become tame while coming into camps for salt are a setup when hunting season arrives, and heavily used licks become holes two to three feet deep.

The biggest stock management problem you face is holding your stock in camp.

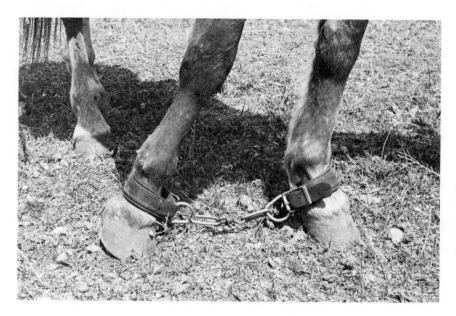

Figure 101. Hobbled horses quickly learn to move around and can cover many miles in a surprisingly short time.

Here again no solution is perfect, and you will have to work out a system that suits you and works for your animals. Animals differ in their tendency to drift away. Some are born explorers, and nothing short of penning or tying them is going to keep them around camp. Others you couldn't drive away.

The best system for ensuring your animals get enough to eat, while minimizing the chances of injury and holding down range damage, is simply to turn all your stock loose. This is what Smoke does. He keeps two or three horses on foot pickets in case the herd drifts away overnight. The rest are turned loose without hobbles, after bells are hung on the dominant horses. These are horses that other horses and mules tend to follow. You can find out which of your horses are dominant by watching who is in the lead when they come in from pasture to be fed. Large strings may have sub-groups, each with its own leader, often a mare. A quick way to sort out the pecking order is to throw a bale of hay to the whole string in a small corral and watch who gets to eat. It's best to form your conclusions from both types of observation since some horses who dominate food are loners, not leaders.

The problem with turning horses loose is obvious — they can be gone in a hurry. The chances of this happening seem to be greater with small strings and strings that go infrequently into the mountains. While Smoke's string figures that home is

wherever it happens to be that night, yours will remember all too clearly where you parked the truck. A larger herd, too, seems to have a certain inertia, and a single restless animal is less likely to get everyone stirred up and moving than he is in a string of three or four. Very few amateurs turn all their stock loose.

Most recreational packers use some combination of hobbles, pickets, bells and prayer. Hobbles are probably the most popular restraint, but they are far from foolproof. Animals quickly get used to moving around in hobbles. They develop a peculiar hopping gait, rearing slightly to advance their front feet then walking with their hind feet to catch up. Some very coordinated horses can actually canter while hobbled, and nearly any horse will eventually learn to move well enough to cover many miles while you sleep.

Another drawback is that an animal, unused to hobbles, can sore his ankles badly. This may not lame him, but the fetlocks will swell and fester, and during fly season the open sores that result can be slow to heal. In bad cases the fetlocks may be permanently disfigured. Some people attempt to avoid this problem by putting hobbles above the ankles. This saves fetlocks at the expense of tendons. Once a horse has learned to be hobbled, he won't hurt himself regardless of where you put them. If you want to use hobbles, let your horses learn to be hobbled at home with you watching. Start by leaving them on for short

Figure 102. One
of Smoke's
foot pickets.

periods only. Keep hobbles well-oiled and soft.

The third and most serious problem with hobbles is that they can be dangerous in brushy or timbered country. A hobbled horse who leaves camp may trip and injure himself or get hung up on a fallen tree. In either case, you may never find him, and he'll slowly starve to death. Bells reduce this danger slightly, but hobbled horses should never be left out over night in timbered areas.

As an alternative to hobbles, both Smoke and I prefer to picket by a front foot. A good single foot picket is pictured in Figure 102. The foot strap is simply half of a hobble. This should be oiled until soft and can even be covered with a sleeve of artificial fleece (also pictured). Attached to the hobble is an eight foot length of smooth chain. Unlike rope, this won't kink or form standing loops on the ground that might catch a foot. Also the chain won't cause rope burns on a horse's rear pasterns as rope often does. The rope is simply a 33 foot manty or sling rope which saves carrying an extra piece of equipment. Tie it to the swivel on the screw-in stake with a bowline so that it can be easily untied later. Screw-in stakes, made of lightweight alloy, are available for a few dollars in most pet stores. They are admittedly a convenience. A sharpened stake driven into the ground a foot or two will work as well, but after you've manufactured and pounded stakes for a few days, you'll appreciate being able to screw a

pin into the ground. Picketing to trees is hard on the trees and more trouble than it's worth. Inevitably the animal will succeed in winding himself up tight against the trunk and you'll get very tired of running out to unwind him.

The Forest Service doesn't like packers to picket stock. They maintain that picketed animals do more damage to the range than loose or hobbled animals. That's often true, but it needn't be. When you picket an animal, move him often. Twice a day isn't too often. At the very least, move him any time you can see the circle where he's been feeding.

Picketing, like hobbling, should be taught at home. An animal who panics his first time on a picket can hurt himself badly, possibly even breaking a leg. If you follow this routine, you should have no problems: The first day put on only the single hobble half and let him walk around in a corral or

Figure 103.
Accustom your stock
to being caught.

pen until he's used to having it flopping around on his ankle. When he's ignoring this, you can add the chain or the rope, and lead him around until he's used to it dragging behind his ankles. It's important to do this in a small pen or corral so that if he bolts, he won't get away and start running dragging a loose rope that might catch on something and throw him. Once he's used to the rope, you can picket him to something solid, like a snubbing post, but tie him short — three to six feet is plenty — so that if he fights, he can't get up enough speed or force to hurt himself. Actually, if you've gone through all the other steps, he's unlikely to blow up at this point. Once he understands how he's restrained, you can gradually lengthen the picket.

Picketed animals, even experienced ones, should always be led to the end of their picket rope before you leave them. An animal who hasn't felt himself restrained either may not realize that he's tied or may not know where his rope will stop him. If he spooks or tries to move after a bunch of loose stock, he may hurt himself.

Picketing from a foot is much safer than picketing by the head or neck. If a shod animal starts scratching an ear with a hind foot and a shoe hooks on his halter, you and your horse or mule have a problem. For the same reason, we don't like to leave any unattended horse or mule, whether hobbled, loose or picketed, with a halter on. A loose animal with a halter on is just as loose as one without a halter, and no easier to catch.

Life will be more pleasant if you accustom your animals to being caught. As the owner of a small string, you're in a much better position to do this than a professional packer who owns 30 or 40 head. At home I make a point of walking up to my horses from time to time for no particular reason except to keep them used to it and to keep them a little off balance. Greed is a powerful horse and mule emotion. Most are suckers for a treat, and I exploit this weakness. Sometimes I feed them a few pellets; sometimes I don't. Sometimes I catch and halter them; sometimes I don't. If they don't know whether they're going to get something to eat or not, they are less likely to run off on the slim chance that I want to ride them. In the hills I do the same thing, carrying pellets in my pockets and walking up to them whenever they're around. When I catch them, I halter them before they get any pellets. That way, there's a little incentive for sticking their noses in the halter.

We don't want to join the endless debate about whether you should be feeding horses treats by hand. We don't tolerate nipping, and neither should you. Also, don't feed treats every time you walk up to a

Figure 104.
A picket line.
Notice the bare
rocky ground.
On such a site
there will be
little damage
from trampling.

horse or mule. Behavioral psychologists learned long ago that rats learn more rapidly when they're rewarded on a random schedule than when the right behavior pays off every time. That seems to be true when it comes to catching stock. We don't feed horses and mules by hand to make pets out of them or to make them like us. Forget such sentimentality. The best horse in the world is worthless in the hills if he won't be caught.

We said you'd have to work out your own system for grazing your stock in the hills, but if you're completely new to packing, you need a place to start. Try this: if you have mules and they live with your saddle horses, turn them loose. Mules rarely will leave horses that they run with. Picket one saddle horse for security. If one horse proves to be an unregenerate traveler who heads for home the minute your back is turned, he's the one to picket; nothing else will keep him in camp. Otherwise you can picket a different horse each day. Picketing a mare, particularly a mare proven to be a group leader, will keep your geldings in camp. Turn the rest of your horses loose, belling the leaders. Hobble only horses that are hard to catch and then only during the day.

At first you probably will sleep better if you bring your stock in and tie or corral them before you go to bed. Later you may want to experiment with leaving some loose all night. When my wife's mare is picketed, my gelding isn't going anywhere. He tends to loose weight quickly on a pack trip and night-long grazing keeps him fit.

Most packers tie their stock to trees. The Forest Service justifiably frowns on this practice and tries to discourage it. They argue that tied horses and mules paw and trample root systems, and in popular camp sites will eventually kill trees. This sort of damage can be minimized if you construct a picket line. This is nothing more than a strong rope — several sling ropes tied together work fine — strung between two or more trees. Picket lines won't eliminate trampling and pawing, but they will reduce it, and they let you control where it occurs. The best picket line sites are gravelly areas with little vegetation. Next best are lodgepole stands. By tying the first horse six feet or so from the tree, you virtually eliminate root damage. Because horses are social animals who like to be with their fellows, horses and mules tied on a picket line will stand more quietly with less nervous pawing than animals tied singly to trees.

Picket ropes should be chest high, about three feet above the ground, to discourage animals from stepping over or under it. Animals should be tied very short to the picket line and on alternate sides about eight feet apart to eliminate fighting.

Makeshift corrals are possible and permissible but can be more trouble than they're worth. The simplest is simply a single strand rope corral, but its ability to hold hungry stock for any length of time is severely suspect. A more sophisticated version of the rope corral uses electric tape powered by lantern batteries to make an electric fence. Neither of us has tried one of these systems so we can't comment on their efficiency. However, they mean carrying extra equipment and, in our opinion, represent an unnecessary importation of technology into the wilderness.

Drift fences can provide a little extra security should your string strike off down the trail when you're not looking. Drift fences are usually makeshift rail gates constructed across narrow places in the trail on either side of many popular camps. In designated wilderness areas where permanent structures are forbidden, drift gates have a dubious role, though calling them "permanent" invests them with a stature most sorely lack. We don't feel that you should add to the proliferation of such fences, but neither do we feel you should go around destroying them or even ignoring them where they exist. Drift gates are plentiful, and without seriously inconveniencing anyone, they can add considerably to your peace of mind while your stock grazes.

A more acceptable alternative is living drift fences. In camps where the stock might be tempted to go for a midnight stroll, wranglers sleep near the inbound and outbound trails where, at least in theory, the horse bells will wake them in time to head the herd back where it belongs.

If in spite of everything, you do wake up some morning to find some or all of your stock has wandered off, there are some things you can do that will save you a lot of frantic searching and improve your chances of finding the prodigals quickly. First, don't panic. If everyone rushes off in a different direction, you may find your horses and lose some of your friends. Plan your search. Decide who is going where, and even more important, decide how long to keep looking before you regroup. Before you walk twenty miles to the trailhead, you want to make sure that someone else didn't find the stock on the other side of camp.

The tinkle of horse bells can keep you from riding past strays that are holing up in the shade, but tracks are the single best friend you have. Look for them on the trails, and try the return trail first. Most of the time, stock that leaves a camp, intent on going somewhere, will leave on the trail and will head back toward the trailhead or a previous camp. If you don't find tracks on the trail within a mile of camp in either direction, go back and concentrate your search in the meadows around camp. The old jokers probably haven't gone anywhere. They're hiding from flies back in the trees or out of sight on a bench up the hill.

If you should find stock on the trail ahead of you, drop off the trail and circle wide to get ahead of them. By continuing down the trail hoping to catch up, you'll only drive them ahead of you.

Although we make these suggestions in the hope they'll save you time, worry and trouble, we tend toward the fatalistic view that when it comes to finding lost animals, no amount of advice will spare you your allotted portion of bitter but instructive experience.

On Smoke's first trip this past spring, a group of us woke to find our eight mules gone. The saddle stock was tied to trees, but the horse I had been riding had been picketed and had pulled his stake and gone with the mules. Four of us saddled up to go looking while Smoke scouted the trail for tracks, and by the time we were mounted, he'd found where the mules had entered the trail, apparently headed toward the trailhead twelve miles back. The other three riders loped off after them.

With my saddle horse gone, I had saddled the only pack horse in the string, and I regretted it immediately. Strength and steadiness were his virtues, and in spite of his best ground pounding efforts, I was soon far behind. A mile down the trail it struck me that I hadn't seen a mule print in quite a while — mule prints are U-shaped, while horses leave an oval track — but the trail was narrow, and I half convinced myself that the three riders ahead were obliterating any fresh tracks.

Another mile and my faith in my companion's tracking ability was wavering. There were no mule tracks across a wide boggy spot, so I kicked the old pack horse into a lumber — you could hardly call it a lope — until I caught the others. I told them that I thought we'd missed the mules somewhere outside of camp and that I was going back to look. They could go on if they wanted to. They did.

It was going to be embarrassing enough to get back and find the mules in camp without adding the agony of riding an unnecessary 25 miles.

The mules, of course, were waiting when I got back. Smoke had seen them on the hill just as we'd galloped off, but in the excitement of the chase, no one had heard him yell to us. If we'd continued watching the ground, instead of deciding on the basis of a few tracks that the mule's were headed for the road, we'd have seen where they left the trail, and we'd have saved ourselves a lot of trouble and embarrassment.

After unsaddling, I joined the others by the coffee pot, and, in an effort to save face, I described how, after two miles, I had concluded correctly that we were on a wild mule chase.

"Jeez," Smoke interrupted. "You mean it took you two miles to realize there weren't any mule tracks?"

I admitted lamely that it had.

"I don't know," Smoke went on, "no matter how many times I tell you, you guys insist on learning the hard way that you always, always find lost horses in their last tracks."

chapter nine
Our Last Tracks

We are now in our last tracks, and rather than leave you with one more technique or morsel of packer's lore, we want to give you some things to think about while you're packing. Anything more that we might tell you about packing would be frosting. We've passed along what we think are our best ideas, and in the process we've given you the basics you need to start packing and a good deal more. If you still want to be a packer, it's time to stop reading and go out and pack.

If it hasn't hit you by now, it soon will — packing isn't very hard. The technical part isn't anyway. Even though things won't work out quite right at first, with a little practice, anyone who can find his or her way around a horse can learn to fit a pack saddle and attach loads to it.

Still, packing is a skill, and if it is not quite an art, it is at least a craft. There are good packers and bad packers. Yet the world has changed — grown more crowded and less wild — and with it the craft of packing has changed too. Once packing was purely a practical matter, no more inspiring or romantic than driving a cross-country semi. But since it has become a form of recreation, packing has taken on new aspects. What separates good packers from bad packers is no longer who can throw a faster diamond hitch. There are poor packers who can "sure enough jerk a rope" and good packers who agonize over every manty. Today, two things set apart the good packer — the way he cares for and uses his stock, and the way he treats the land.

A packer's horses and mules are neither pets nor machines. They are living creatures who's work earns them protection and care. An amateur packer's animals have no function but to further their owner's pleasure, and pleasure is the only measure of performance. There is no other; not miles walked, hours or days worked, or money earned. It should be a matter of principle and pride to bring your horses and mules out of the hills in as good or better condition than they went in.

Your relationship as a packer to the country you travel in is similar but more complex. That relationship is reflected in how you behave in the backcountry. When you go into wilderness looking for peace, beauty, adventure or reacquaintance with an increasingly removed natural world, you assume — like it or not — the mantle of a steward of that country. There is no place for a let-Joe-do-it attitude. There is no Joe. If you say, "My taxes support the Forest Service or the Park Service or the Bureau of Land Management... Where's the trash barrel?" you're simply bringing with you a selfish detachment that is all too typical in our society. You might as well stay home.

a.

Figure 105a-c.
Packing isn't very hard.

has suggested that if you need incentive to clean up after yourself, you should pretend that you're a criminal (that shouldn't be hard because you are), and every poptop and gum wraper left along your route, even if they aren't yours, hastens the day when you'll be caught. Prison for us is a place far away from wild country, an impersonal, dead world of concrete and steel and antiseptic smells, that mask decay and filth. Sound like many big cities? That should be

b.

c.

(Smoke says, "Please do.")

If you feel inclined to make a fetish out of some aspect of packing, make it minimum impact camping, not equipment, obscure hitches or high-bred stock. You don't have to tear up the country to have a comfortable camp. The more you modify your campsite, the further you push back the very wilderness you came to experience. Smoke proves day after day that it is possible to camp even with large groups of inexperienced people and up to 25 head of stock, and leave only a little flattened grass where the tents stood to show he was there. You should be able to do at least as well.

To benefit from the mountains and from wild places, you have to care about them enough to care for them. If you do, then you don't need lectures from us. If you don't care, responsible behavior is going to be hard for you. A forest ranger Smoke knows

146

*Figure 106.
Early in this century,
packing became
a form of recreation.*

incentive enough. But then you shouldn't
need incentive.

As a horse packer, you are the only
wilderness user equipped to leave the
mountains cleaner than you found them. It
costs almost nothing in time and effort to
pack out trash you find in your camps and
along the way. Yet there is more to
wilderness degradation than trash, and
more to clean camping than cosmetics.

Packing unavoidably has a great impact
on the country simply because horses and
mules are big animals who trample things
and have to eat. Packers have to accept this
and make every effort to minimize the
effects of their passing. How to do this
without degrading the unique character of
the pack trip experience is the most
pressing question facing packers, both
amateur and professional, today.

On the one hand are those advocating
technological and logistical solutions —
packing all food for both humans and stock,
electrically fenced temporary corrals,
gasoline or propane stoves instead of open
fires, restrictions on user numbers,
controlled itineraries, filed weeks or
months in advance.... Opposed to this

approach are those like ourselves, who
believe that a traditional style is an
important, indeed an essential part of a
satisfying wilderness experience. We
believe, perhaps idealistically, that the
need to preserve the untrammeled
character of the backcountry and the
freedoms it represents is best served
without recourse to technology or excessive
regulation.

Our vision can only prevail if packers
accept their responsibility to the
wilderness, remaining always conscious of
the damage they can do and taking every
care to minimize it. Packers must accept the
dictum "Take only pictures; leave only
footprints.." with the same fervor and
unanimity as the backpackers who coined
it. And they must extend courtesy,
consideration and tolerance to other
wilderness users. All this will mean the
demise of some traditional practices still in
use, but these need not be replaced by
technological substitutes. To the greatest
extent possible comfort and amenity must
depend on skill rather than on equipment or
exploitation. The alternative is to be
registered, regulated, allocated and

Figure 107.
*Your relationship
to the country is
reflected in how
you behave in the
backcountry.
No packing skill is
more important.*

ultimately unsatisfied.

Lest we leave you on too negative a note, we want to remind you that packing is fun. It has provided us with as much enjoyment as anything we have ever done.

Nearly a year has passed since we began to assemble this book. I think we were moved to begin it, in part, because it was spring in the valleys and we were eager to ride somewhere. But there was still too much snow in the high country to pack, so we did the next best thing — we talked about it, and the talks became a book.

This past winter has been unusually mild. Already whiffs of spring are wafting across shrinking drifts. The hill behind Smoke's is bare of snow, and I find myself eyeing my barefoot horses, wondering whether, if I should dare to tack on shoes, winter would return with a vengeance. Despite the fact that June and open high country trails are months away... despite his nearly quarter of a century packing, Smoke is growing as restless as I am.

Perhaps we'll pass you on the trail this summer in the Danaher, on the Sun River, under the Chinese Wall, catching big cutthroat on the South Fork....

When is all that snow going to melt?

Good riding.

Figure 108. The best – and for most people the
only – reason for packing is to have fun.

APPENDIX I
A Planning Guide for an
8-day Pack Trip for 4 People

EQUIPMENT LIST

4 saddle horses, including halters, bridles, saddle pads or blankets and riding saddles

3 pack horses or mules, including halters, pack saddles and saddle pads or blankets

6 manties & ropes

	Approx. weight
2 two-man tents (preferably tall enough to stand up in) with poles, or	22 lbs.
1 10x12 wall tent	32 lbs.
1 12x12 fly, plastic or light nylon	4 lbs.

Kitchen equipment packed in waxed cardboard meat box with lid:
   1 12" skillet
   1 light griddle 8"x12"
   1 1-qt., 2 2-qt., & 1 4-qt. pans with lids
   1 coffee pot
   1 teapot
   2 metal dishpans
   1 metal wash pan
   6 plates
   6 knives, forks & spoons
   6 cups that will stack
   4 large serving or mixing spoons
   1 spatula
   1 large butcher knife
   1 small paring knife
   1 canopener
   1 wire whisp
   1 flat grater
   1 corkscrew
   2 buckets, plastic or canvas
   1 tablecloth
   4 or 5 dish towels.   48 lbs.

Stove or 20"x30" grill with pipe   12-32 lbs.

4 sleeping pads or air mattresses with repair kit & pump   6-25 lbs.

1 first-aid kit (see p. 92)   5 lbs.

1 horse first-aid kit (see p. 93)   5 lbs.

1 horseshoe rasp and 1 Easy Boot ™ (sized to fit your stock)   3 lbs.

2 20"x36"x½" pieces of plywood (table at camp)   6 lbs.

1 Repair kit:
   screwdriver
   pliers
   2 snaps
   tape
   wire
   rivets
   16 horseshoe nails
   lantern generator
   extra mantles
   flat file
             8 lbs.

1 gas lantern or large battery lantern with gas in fuel bottle or extra battery   3 lbs.

1 pole axe — 36" handle with scabbard   3 lbs.

1 shovel — 42" handle with scabbard   2 lbs.

1 bow saw with scabbard   1½ lbs.

3 bells with throat straps   6 lbs.

2 picket straps & chains with picket pins   6 lbs.

4 sleeping bags & personal gear* — including fishing & hunting gear   100 lbs.

Horse ration, pellets or grain (½ complete ration — 3 lbs. per horse per day with some grazing)   150 lbs.

4 nose bags   5 lbs.

1 4-lb. block of salt   4 lbs.

Optional

1 toilet set   5 lbs.

4 camp stools   5 lbs.

       Total   400-460 lbs.

* See personal equipment list in chapter four.

MENUS

The following are typical meal-plans that Smoke uses:

BREAKFASTS

Bacon & Eggs
or
Small Breakfast Steaks & Eggs
or
Sausage & Eggs

Hotcakes
or
French Toast
(especially if you're long on bread)

Juice or Fresh Fruit In Season

Coffee

LUNCHES

Sandwich Assortments:
Cold Cuts • Cheese
Peanut Butter • Jelly
Tuna-Egg Mixture

Cookies and/or Candy Bar
Orange or Apple

Hot Soup
(on cool layover days in camp)

DINNERS

one
Meatballs & Gravy
Mashed Potatoes
Three-bean Salad
Corn
Cake & Coffee

Substitutes for the meatballs could be Swiss steak or roast beef, pre-cooked almost to the finish point – so that this first day when the cook could be rushed, dinner can be on the table fast. Pre-cooked meats are steamed in covered pan. Liquid becomes gravy base. Three-bean salad is prepared at home.

two
Chicken & Rice
Green Beans
Tossed Salad
Canned Fruit
Coffee

The chicken is pre-cooked. Smoke uses only chicken breasts, eliminating the bulk and waste of other pieces that have less meat and more bone.

three
Pork Chops & Applesauce
Stuffing with Wild Rice
Peas
Chocolate Pudding
Coffee

four
Cube Steaks
Mashed Potatoes
Carrots
Tossed Salad
Banana Bread
Coffee

five
Casserole
*(such as Tuna Helper,
spaghetti or stew)*
Tossed Salad
Green Vegetable
Vanilla Pudding
Coffee

In place of fresh meat in spaghetti sauce, substitute protein granules (soybean). They are available in bacon, ham or hamburger flavor and in a spaghetti sauce are nearly indistinguishable from hamburger. They weigh far less, and should you happen to have one evening meal of trout, you can eliminate the spaghetti without wasting fresh meat.

six
Sirloin Steak
Mashed Potatoes
Peas & Carrots
Tossed Salad
Fruit
Coffee

seven
Fried Ham
Mashed Potatoes
Butter Beans
Pineapple/Cucumber Tossed Salad
Butterscotch Pudding
Coffee

Pre-cook all meats that tend to spoil fast, or plan to use them early in your trip. Double wrap all meat and freeze it solid. Prior to boxing the meat in a waxed cardboard box, wrap it in newspaper for further insulation. Other perishables, such as cottage cheese, mayonaise, etc., can be packed among the frozen meats.

GROCERY LIST
for the preceding menus.

MEAT

1½ lb. hamburger, 1 lb. pork sausage (for about 14 meatballs)

8 chicken breasts

8 thick cut pork chops

4 6-oz. sirloin steaks

8 ¼"-thick slices of frying ham (save for last night — this keeps very well)

3 lbs. bacon (6 or more adequate breakfasts)

1 lb. link sausage (or four small breakfast steaks)

4 lbs. assorted lunch meat (wrap in 1 lb. packages, approximately 10 slices per pound — remember, a package once opened spoils faster)

1½ lbs. hamburger for spaghetti or soy-based meat substitute or 2 9¼-oz. cans tuna for tuna casserole

1 9¼-oz. can tuna for emergency sandwich making

FRUITS & VETETABLES — A 16-oz. can of most vegtables will serve 4.

1 16-oz. can corn — or do as Smoke does and substitute ½ cup freeze-dried corn

2 16-oz. cans green beans — substitute ¾-1 cup freeze-dried beans

1 16-oz. can peas & carrots — substitute ½ cup freeze-dried peas and carrots

1 16-oz. can peas — substitute ½ cup freeze-dried peas

2 cans butter beans

1 16-oz. can carrots — substitute ½ cup freeze-dried carrots

dried potatoes — (Smoke favors the Carnation brand Trio potato powder — 1½-2 cups of powder more than adequately serve 4)

1 28-oz. can peaches — substitute 1½-2 cups freeze-dried peaches

1 16-oz. can pineapple (10 slices)

1 16-oz. can pineapple chunks (to use in salad)

1 16-oz. can fruit cocktail (to mix with vanilla pudding)

1 6-oz. can green beans, 1 6-oz. can wax beans, 1 6-oz. can pinto beans (for 3-bean salad)

CANNED STAPLES

½ gallon maple syrup (or dry mix or mapeline & extra sugar)

1 lb. jar peanut butter

1 1-qt. jar jelly (repack in light-weight plastic jars)

1 pint mayonaise (remember hot days, long rides and mayonaise make a dangerous combination — save unopened for days when you're making lunch right before eating it.

1 small jar mustard (repack into Gerry™ tube)

1 small bottle catsup (repack into Gerry™ tube)

1 small jar pickles (repack into light-weight plastic jar)

2 lbs. of coffee (resack using double plastic bags)

1 box of tea bags

1 can of hot chocolate mix

Kool-Aide or ice tea mix (plan on enough to make 2-4 qts. a day — especially if 2 of the party of 4 are children or non-coffee drinkers)

Orange juice (plan on ½-1 qt. per day — buy a powdered mix and repack in double plastic bags)

SALAD MAKINGS

1 small container of cottage cheese (tape shut and pack with meat or substitute 1½ cups dried cottage cheese)

Dried apples or applesauce mix

4-5 medium heads of lettuce

2 cucumbers, 2 green peppers, small stalk celery, any other fresh vegetables you like in a tossed salad (remember tomatoes are hard to pack)

In recent years, Smoke has started to substitute a wedge of red cabbage, a head of cauliflower, a can or two of garbanzo beans, and a bag of sunflower seeds for some of the more perishable fresh vegetables that are hard to pack.

1 or 2 8-oz. bottles salad dressing of your choice.

DAIRY PRODUCTS

5 dozen eggs provides for 2 eggs per person per day, plus a few extra for french toast or tuna mixture

2 to 2½ lbs. margarine

2 lbs. pre-sliced, individually wrapped cheese slices (these separate easier if they should become a little squashed)

BAKERY ITEMS

1 banana bread

1 small 8x8 cake (the Snack-In-Cakes pack well because they're so moist.

8 loves of bread (Smoke plans an average of 3 slices per day per person — here you may want to substitute pocket bread for 1 or 2 meals since it takes up less space — 3 packages should provide you with 18 sandwiches and take less space than 1 loaf of regular bread)

5-6 dozen cookies

DRIED STAPLES

3 packages pudding mix, chocolate, vanilla & butterscotch

2 3½-lb. sacks of complete hotcake flour

1 lb. sugar (or 2-3 lbs. sugar & bottle of mapeline if you wish to make your own syrup and cut down on unnecessary weight in packing liquid.

Cinnamon, salt & pepper

3 qt. box dried milk

Powdered coffee creamer

MISCELLANEOUS

Package of marshmallows
3 dozen candy bars — substitute granola bars,
    pre-packaged, individual packages of trail mix
    (mixture of raisins, nuts, candy, etc.; make your
    own)
32 apples and/or oranges
1 roll paper towels
1 package of napkins
4 rolls of toilet paper
garbage bags
small roll of foil
matches
small container of biodegradable concentrated dish
    soap
1 bar hand soap

Notes

*For all canned vegetables, you can substitute
freeze-dried. ¼-½ cup of freeze-dried peas or carrots
weighs only 1¼-2 oz. and will feed four. 1 can of peas
or carrots also feeds 4 but weighs 19-20 ozs., and less
than half of that is food. Dried fruit can also be
substituted for canned.*

*There are several good but expensive brands of
freeze-dried food available from local sporting goods*
*stores. If you purchase in small quantities, most
packages are packaged for 2 or 4. Remove outer foil
packaging as it adds considerable bulk.*

*A more reasonable alternative in terms of cost is to
buy dried food in bulk. Two sources that Smoke uses
are a local Neo-Life dealer and Vacu Dry-Utah, Salt
Lake City. Neo-Life offers food packaged in #2½ cans
that can then be packaged according to trip needs.
Vacu-Dry sells in #10 cans and also has a line of
Camplite foods packaged for 2, 4, etc. Well worth
trying are most of their vegetables, fruits, stew mix,
soybean protein granuals, dried syrup, dried cottage
cheese, tomato crystals (great for spaghetti sauce),
dried butter, peanut butter, cheese, applesauce
powder, and potatoes. These products, when
unopened, have a shelf-life of several years.*

*Much packaging outweighs the product it contains.
An empty pickle jar weighs 16-ozs. The contents will
fit in a plastic jar weighing 4-ozs. A 14-oz. empty
bottle of catsup weighs 12-oz. The contents will fit in
a 1½-oz. Gerry tube. Repackaging all dry products
that come in cans or jars — in double plastic bags.
Repackage mayonaise, jellies, mustard, and catsup
into light-weight plastic jars or Gerry tubes.*

*Freeze-dried vegetables or powdered products, when
packaged in plastic bags, have the added advantage
of fitting into the little nooks and crannies in your
grocery box.*

154

Mantying Loads

All livestock that enters the wilderness or the backcountry should be loaded to capacity (1/5th the weight of the animal). This will reduce the number of stock and lessen impact on the environment.

HORSE #ONE

Right side	weight (lbs.)	Left side	weight (lbs.)
1 Tent	11	1 Tent	11
Gear for 2 people	50	Gear for 2 people	50
1 First-aid kit	5	1 Horse first-aid kit	5
2 Air mattresses	12	2 Air mattresses	12
1 20"x36"x½" Plywood	3	1 20"x36"x½" Plywood	3
1 Lantern	3	Horseshoe rasp, etc.	3
12'x12' Fly	4	Repair kit	8
Pole axe	3		
Saw	1½		
	92½ lbs.		92 lbs.

HORSE #TWO

	weight (lbs.)		weight (lbs.)
Kitchen	48	Stove	32
Horse ration	50	2 quarts lantern gas	4
		Bells	6
		Picket	6
		Horse Ration	50
	98 lbs.		98 lbs.

HORSE #THREE

	weight (lbs.)		weight (lbs.)
Food	50	Food	50
Nose bags	5	Stock salt	5
Horse ration	25	Horse ration	25
	80 lbs.		80 lbs.
Optional toilet	5 lbs.	Camp stools	5 lbs.

Note: If grazing conditions make packing feed unnecessary, you can get by with only two pack animals by eliminating the stock ration and combining the loads of horses two and three.

APPENDIX II
Knots

First tie a crown knot.

a.

Unravel about 3 to 4 inches. Fold center strand (1) down to form loop.

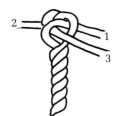

c.

Tighten crown knot by tugging each end in turn. Go around several times to keep the knot even.

Now weave the splice.

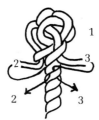

e.

The result of d. Strand 1 disappears in back.

Repeat at least two more times with all three strands (arrows).

Roll between your palms to tighten. You can clip loose ends for appearance, but leaving them protruding can give you a better grip on the end of a lead rope.

BACK SPLICE

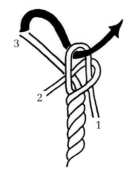

b.

Wrap 2 around loop formed by 1. 2 should pass over 3. Pass 3 through the loop formed by 1.

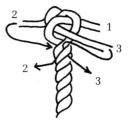

d.

Choose any strand to begin weaving.

Lace it over the strand below, under the strand below that, then out. The arrows show this for strands 2 and 3.

Do this for all three strands. If you become confused, notice that a strand goes in between the twists where the strand to the left comes out. (3 goes under where 2 comes out.)

f.

Back splice woven through 2 cycles. One more will complete it.

EYE-SPLICE

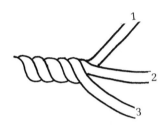

a.

Unravel three to four inches. One strand (in this case 2) will appear as the center strand.

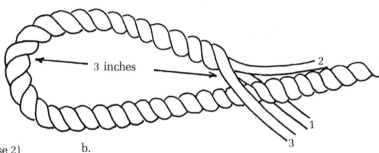

b.

Fold over to form an eye. Three to three and a half inches (the width of four fingers) is a good size.

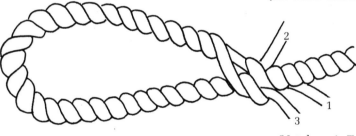

c.

Insert the center strand (2) under any twist of the rope.

Turn splice ⅓ turn so strand 3 is on top and thread it under a twist so that it emerges between the two twists between which 2 was inserted.

(Not shown) Turn splice ⅓ turn more so that strand 1 is on top. It should be inserted between the twists where strand 2 emerges and should emerge between the twists where strand 3 goes in. This is the trickiest step. If you get it right the splice will appear symetrical with all three strands pointing away from the loop and with each emerging between different twists.

d.

From c. it is a simple matter to keep working strands alternately over and under the twists below (exactly like the back splice) until step c. has been repeated at least three times.

Roll the splice under your boot and trim the remaining ends.

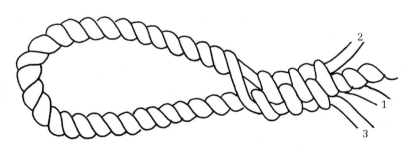

BOWLINE